Jasc® Paint Shop™ Creations

Demystifying Digital Photography

Dave Huss

Jasc Software®

the power to create®

ISBN 0-9745176-0-7

For information, contact:
Jasc Software, Inc.
7905 Fuller Road
Eden Prairie, MN 55344
USA
www.jasc.com

Printed in the United States of America
2003

Contents

Part 2: Taking Better Pictures is Easy 15

Part 3: Organizing and Safeguarding Your Photos 31

Part 4: Working with Non-Digital Images 45

Part 5: Making Your Photos Look Professional ... 67

Part 1

Your Digital Camera

Digital cameras can seem a little intimidating. The first time you open that 100-page quick-start guide (the one printed in five languages) and see all those little parts identified with little balloons (not unlike the silly one I created below with Paint Shop Pro) can be overwhelming.

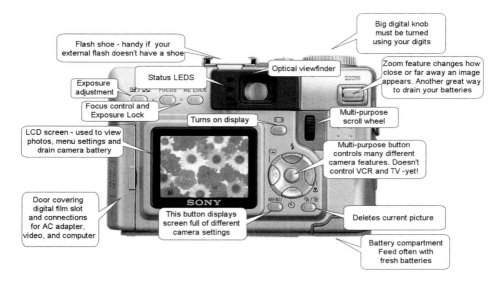

Flash shoe - handy if your external flash doesn't have a shoe

Big digital knob must be turned using your digits

Optical viewfinder

Zoom feature changes how close or far away an image appears. Another great way to drain your batteries

Status LEDS

Exposure adjustment

Focus control and Exposure Lock

Turns on display

Multi-purpose scroll wheel

LCD screen - used to view photos, menu settings and drain camera battery

Multi-purpose button controls many different camera features. Doesn't control VCR and TV -yet!

Door covering digital film slot and connections for AC adapter, video, and computer

This button displays screen full of different camera settings

Deletes current picture

Battery compartment Feed often with fresh batteries

Many digital cameras have a lot of bells and whistles.
(Image courtesy of Sony Electronics)

In the first part of this book we'll cover some digital camera terminology and the features common to most digital cameras. You'll also discover which features are important and which ones are not when buying a digital camera. Lastly we'll consider essential accessories, as well as tips and tricks for vacation travel.

Defining the Digital Camera Categories

Digital cameras are amazing devices. If you take the time to learn how they work internally, you'll quickly realize they are quite powerful. The good news is you don't need to know all that much to use the camera. Digital cameras fall into three general categories:

- Consumer
- Prosumer (professional/consumer)
- Professional, also known as Digital Single Lens Reflex (D-SLR)

Consumer Cameras

Also known as point-and-shoot, consumer cameras make up a large percentage of the digital cameras sold today. While some amateur photographers treat point-and-shoot cameras with contempt, the fact is, the cameras are getting more sophisticated every year. I think there is some resentment about the fact that with one of these cameras, someone with little to no knowledge of photography can produce quality photos. These cameras usually range in price from $200 to $400. Here you can see a few examples of popular consumer digital cameras.

Prosumer Cameras

Typically the prosumer digital camera is the top model offered by a manufacturer. The distinction between the consumer and prosumer camera is blurring, as consumer cameras continue to offer more and more features. At the time of this writing, prosumer cameras offer 5+ megapixels and range in price from $750 to $1,100. While there are about a dozen cameras that can be considered prosumer, the example shown is from Sony.

Digital-SLR (D-SLR)

These cameras look like regular 35mm cameras, because they're built on a camera body derived from the single lens reflex (SLR) camera. When you buy a D-SLR, you're only buying the body. Like the traditional SLR, the lenses on the D-SLR are interchangeable and sold separately. When these cameras first appeared on the market they sold for upwards of $20,000. Today they're in the $900 to $3,000 range (for the camera body alone) with a few high-end models selling for as much as $9,000.

Which Camera is Right For You?

For most people starting out in digital photography, the consumer-level camera is perfect. It's light and small, so it fits easily in pockets or purses. In most situations, the consumer camera does a good job of making a quality image with little to no effort on your part. However, once you learn a few of the techniques described in this book, you'll be taking even better photos than ever before. Soon, taking great photos will become second nature.

In a world with so much technology, we have become conditioned to look for products with the most gadgets. When we buy a digital camera, we often err by getting one with more features than we need. This point was brought home to me when a co-worker offered to sell me his camera. It turned out his wife took most of the photos, and wasn't very happy with the photos the camera was taking. The truth is, the camera had a lot of features and settings that made shooting with it complicated and no fun. So, when you're looking for a digital camera, make sure you get one that fits your style of picture taking.

Digital Camera Anatomy 101

The Camera Sensor

A digital camera captures an image using a sensor. The light sensor found in most digital cameras is called a Charge Coupled Device (CCD). This is the type of device also found in your scanner or office copier. There are other types of sensors (like CMOS), but the CCD is so common many people call all digital camera sensors CCDs — much like how my mother called all refrigerators Frigidaires. No matter what you call it, the sensor has millions of light sensing areas that produce image pixels. The actual resolution of a camera is the total number of pixels located on the CCD sensor. Digital camera resolutions range from 0.3 megapixels to 5+ megapixels. A megapixel is a way of expressing how many pixels are on a CCD sensor in millions. Thus, a 2-megapixel camera has two million pixels on its CCD sensor.

What is a Pixel?

Despite how it sounds, a pixel is not an enchanted winged creature found in fairy tales. Pixels are the building blocks of digital images. Mosaics best illustrate the concept of the pixel. I've included a photo of a mosaic taken in Athens, Greece. If you stand close enough to the image, the individual tiles making up the image are apparent. But, when the mosaic is viewed from a distance it becomes difficult for our eyes to resolve the individual tiles. We just see the shapes and colors of the combined tiles.

The pixels that make up a digital image are like the tiles that make up a mosaic, with one major exception. The tiles in a mosaic have a fixed physical dimension. Pixels are whatever size the output device makes them.

Digital Camera Buying Tip

Before purchasing a digital camera you should determine how much you are willing spend. Then when you get to the store, forget it and buy the camera you want.

Kind of confusing, I know. Here's an example that will help clear things up. The size of the image created by your digital camera is measured in pixels. A popular 3.3-megapixel camera produces an image that is 2048 pixels wide and 1536 pixels tall. So, how large an image will it produce? Since pixels don't have fixed sizes, the resulting image can be as small as a postage stamp or as large as a billboard.

The pixel density (called resolution setting) determines the output size. If Paint Shop Pro tells the output device (color printer) to print the image at a resolution of 2048 pixels-per-inch, the image will be one inch wide. If the image is printed at 100 pixels-per-inch the image will be 20.48 inches wide, as the pixels are made larger to accommodate the lower resolution setting. It's like stepping back from the mosaic. Our eyes cannot resolve the individual pixels and they disappear making the image appear to be made up not of tiny pixels, but a continuous transition of colors and tones. As the resolution decreases and the pixels become larger eventually they become large enough to be noticed and the image appears to be made up of tiny tiles, like the mosaic (this is called pixelation).

Here's a photo of the front grill on an old Dodge. The emblem on the front is how it appears at a normal printing resolution of approximately 200 pixels-per-inch (which is incorrectly called dots-per-inch by everyone). This image, when printed, will be about four inches wide.

What if I needed to make it four times larger? I could just change the image's resolution using Paint Shop Pro's resize command. Now that I've changed the resolution to 50 pixels-per-inch, when the image is printed it will be 16 inches wide, but at a lower resolution the pixels will be larger (since there are fewer pixels-per-inch they don't have to be as small). The larger pixels would begin to make themselves known as I've shown in the close-up of the emblem. You'll learn more about image resizing as we work on different projects. For now, just remember that pixels are the building blocks of digital images.

How Big Does the Sensor Need To Be?

As of this writing, the 4-megapixel digital cameras are the most popular. Whether you're photographing real estate for a Web site or taking family snapshots, if you get a camera with a sensor between 3 and 4 megapixels, it'll be more than sufficient. I recently read an article in a photo magazine where the author pointed out the inadequacy of the 3-megapixel camera because it won't make acceptable 11 x 17 inch (tabloid) photos. Most of us shouldn't worry about this. When's the last time (other than wedding photos) you've wanted an image that large? Consider what you normally shoot and, unless you have a side business in wedding photography, stick with a 3 or 4-megapixel camera. Now that the sensor question has been answered, let's talk some about the other important features to consider.

Digital Camera Buying Tip

Don't buy for the future. Many people I talk with bought a camera with features they don't need or use. They bought the camera with the idea they're going to stick with it for many years and grow into the features. While this is a good philosophy for a food blender, digital camera technology changes too rapidly. Buy as much camera as you're going to use today, and wait until you actually out-grow it to get one with all the bells and whistles.

Zoom Factor

Question: What's generally advertised in the form of a giant sticker on the outside of the digital camera box?

Answer: The second most important feature of a digital camera — the zoom factor.

When it comes to zoom factors, you want the biggest number possible. A greater zoom factor means your camera has a larger range of magnification. But it's a bit trickier than that. There are two types of zoom — optical and digital. One expensive camera has a big sticker on the box that declares "12x zoom." The fact is, the camera is fitted with a 4x optical zoom lens and also adds an additional 3x digital zoom (4x3=12x zoom). When looking at zoom, you want a camera with a large optical zoom — that's what really counts.

Tip

Many digital cameras automatically engage the digital zoom when you zoom the camera out to its maximum focal length. I strongly suggest you read your manual and find out what menu setting turns off the digital zoom feature so it doesn't accidentally engage.

The Importance of Zoom — Optical vs. Digital

Optical zoom is produced by the lens system and is the magnification difference between minimum (wide angle) and maximum (telephoto) focal lengths. Digital zoom crops to the center part of the image and enlarges it. Photos taken with optical zoom look good, while images made using digital zoom tend to show pixelation. The top image shown to the right used digital zoom. Pretty ugly.

The image below it was taken with the same camera at roughly the same distance using optical zoom. Any questions?

Using your camera's digital zoom feature (above) usually results in degraded photos

Viewfinders and LCD Screens

Most digital cameras have an optical viewfinder and a flat LCD screen on the back. The LCD can be used to compose photos as well as to review the photos you've just taken. On a bright, sunny day the chance of actually using the LCD to compose a shot is next to impossible, because you can't see anything. In such cases you can use the optical viewfinder to compose the photo. Some of the most expensive cameras offer an electronic view-

Restricting your camera to optical zoom produces superior images

finder that operates much like the optical viewfinder. You put your eye up to the viewfinder and when you look through it you see the image that also appears on the LCD. Although it's much smaller than the LCD on the back of your camera, it can be viewed clearly on the brightest day.

Some cameras offer articulated LCD screens like the ones that are so common on camcorders. These screens are not fixed to the back of the camera; they swivel around giving you greater versatility when composing photos. Articulated LCD screens allow you to take pictures from all angles. For instance, you can hold the camera above your head and compose the photo while looking up into the LCD screen you've turned around.

Using an articulated LCD screen while taking pictures of children is my favorite. I place the camera on a table, which lets me talk to the child face to face while composing the photo by watching the LCD out of the corner of my eye.

Digital Film

First of all, digital film isn't film at all. Rather it's the removable storage device where your digital camera stores the images you take. Digital film is called by many names, including (but not limited to) memory, memory card, and removable media. In the past, the type of media (digital film) your camera used was an important question. Once there were several competing technologies, much like when VHS and Beta-Max fought for the videotape market 20 years ago.

Today, the storage media used by most digital cameras is Compact Flash (CF). Sony and a few other companies use a Memory Stick™, and while it has gained some in popularity, the market is pretty much settled on CF. Still, you'll run into several different memory devices, so a quick summary will be helpful.

Compact Flash (CF)

At the moment, CF cards are the dominant choice in digital film. CF offers the greatest amount of storage at the lowest price. The largest capacity CF card can store a whopping 4GB worth of images. One point about CF cards that can be confusing to some digital camera owners has to do with the card's speed. Lexar, for example, advertises a 40x write speed. Speed refers to how fast the memory can receive images from the camera. Here's the part that you might not have known: there's no difference in speed when these cards are used in consumer cameras. Only on professional cameras (the ones that cost thousands of dollars) will a speed difference be noticed.

Memory Stick (MS)

Roughly the same size as a stick of gum, the MS is slowly gaining in popularity. It's starting to appear in devices other than those made by Sony. Up until recently, the capacity of the MS was limited to 128MB. The new MS Pro can offer

capacities up to 1GB. You should be aware that these larger capacity sticks might not work on older devices.

Multi-Media Card (MMC) and Secure Digital (SD)

The MMC was designed to fit into everything digital from PDAs and cell phones, to MP3 players and digital cameras. This format is gaining in popularity as it can serve as the go between for all those portable electronic devices we can no longer seem to live without. SD is a variation of MMC that has an erasure-prevention switch to keep your data safe. When the switch is in the locked position, it will stop you from accidentally copying over or deleting any data stored on your card. There are some digital cameras that can use MMC, but CF is still the most popular media.

SmartMedia

This is the removable media that lost the war to CF. At this time only Olympus still supports SmartMedia. Most media vendors are either no longer making SmartMedia, or have quit making new, higher capacity versions.

xD-Picture Card

At the moment this media is only found on Olympus cameras. While this newest digital media has a lot of potential, the fact is, until it's more widely used by other camera manufacturers the selection of both capacity and price will be limited.

A Checklist for Digital Camera Buyers

Here's a summary of camera features in order of importance:

- **Sensor Size** — Any camera between 3 and 4 megapixels will work just fine. If you get a great bargain on a 2+-megapixel camera, snap it up. You'll still get good results.

- **Zoom Factor** — Always try to get the greatest optical zoom factor you can afford.

- **LCD Screen and Electronic Viewfinder** — If possible, get a camera with an articulated LCD screen and an electronic viewfinder. Don't break the bank getting these features, but if you can get them, they're awfully nice.

- **Media** — As a rule, a camera that uses Compact Flash will allow you to get the best bargains when buying additional memory cards. Memory Stick is second and MMC/SD is third. Give a lot of thought to buying a camera that uses any of the other media, xD

Picture Card or SmartMedia, as you might paint yourself into a virtual corner when it comes time to get additional media.

Essential Digital Camera Accessories

If you buy your digital camera from a camera salesperson, he/she is probably going to try to upgrade the sale by having you buy accessories. Since the person recommending that you buy additional equipment ultimately benefits from the sale, there's a chance their advice isn't always in your best interest. So, since I can't sell you anything and you already have this book, I'll give you a prioritized list of essential digital camera accessories.

Rechargeable Batteries

Digital cameras eat batteries for lunch — and dinner. Between the LCD screen and the motorized zoom mechanism the expected life span of a battery in a digital camera isn't long. An associate I work with bought a camera just like mine last year. After a week I asked him how he liked the camera. "It's a great camera but goes through batteries pretty quickly," he said. It turned out he went to a family reunion and over two days went through five sets of AA batteries — I guess they don't keep going and going and going.

The problem was, his camera shipped from the manufacturer with a fresh set of alkaline batteries, making him think that's what he had to use. If we hadn't talked, I'm sure he'd have been receiving Christmas cards from the local battery outlet. So let's talk a little about batteries and what kind to use.

Many consumer cameras use four standard AA batteries. To meet the power demands of the digital camera, you should buy two sets of rechargeable Nickel-Hydride batteries (NiMH) and a charger. Some of the more expensive cameras use a custom battery designed specifically for the camera. While it means that getting a second battery isn't as easy as stopping by the local store, the positive side is that these batteries tend to be Lithium-Ion (Li) and typically have a longer life span. I shoot a Nikon D-100 (D-SLR) and the battery is good for almost 1,000 photos. As a result, when I go on a photo shoot I only carry one spare battery. When I use one of my cameras with AA batteries, I have to carry several spare sets.

Battery Chargers

Your choice of a battery charger deserves a little consideration. The physical properties of NiMH batteries are different than ordinary alkaline, and you'll need a charger designed to charge NiMH batteries. I recommend getting a charger that will rapidly charge batteries (it usually takes about 90 minutes). A slow trickle charger takes closer to 15 hours. The cost difference is small and your time is worth more. Plus, the slow charger actually reduces the life of the NiMH batteries.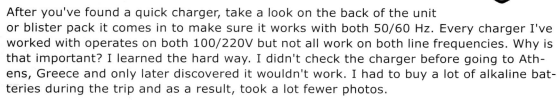

After you've found a quick charger, take a look on the back of the unit or blister pack it comes in to make sure it works with both 50/60 Hz. Every charger I've worked with operates on both 100/220V but not all work on both line frequencies. Why is that important? I learned the hard way. I didn't check the charger before going to Athens, Greece and only later discovered it wouldn't work. I had to buy a lot of alkaline batteries during the trip and as a result, took a lot fewer photos.

Ensuring the long, healthy life of NiMH batteries

Don't drop the batteries on the ground; they tend to be more fragile than alkaline batteries.
After charging, the batteries will be warm, let them cool down before putting them in your camera.

NiMH batteries don't suffer from the "memory effect" that NiCad batteries experience, no matter what the person at the camera store tells you.

Mobile Chargers

If you do a lot of traveling by car, you may want to consider a power converter. It produces AC power from the cigarette lighter socket in your vehicle. Most converters today cost less than $25 and if your camera came with a charger, it works great on a long trip.

Extra Memory

Most media cards for digital cameras are becoming quite reasonable. With 128MB CF cards approaching the $25 mark, you don't have to try to pack your entire 10-day vacation on a 64MB card by setting your resolution to low quality.

Because the really large media cards are the most expensive, you should shop around to find the best price for your media. For example, I use CF cards. Today, I can get a 128MB card for $25, a 256MB for $55, and a 512MB for $149. If I buy two 256MB cards, I only pay $110 for 512MB of storage, instead of $149.

Optional Accessories

So far, I've listed the accessories most digital camera users would consider essential. Beyond that, there are many more accessories and add-ons than you can imagine. Below I will list a few optional accessories that are practical and expand what you can do with your camera.

Polarizer Filter

A polarizer filter allows you to remove unwanted reflections from non-metallic surfaces such as water and glass. This filter also makes colors appear more saturated and clearer, with better contrast. This effect is often used to increase the contrast and saturation in blue skies and white clouds without affecting the overall color balance of the shot.

Here's an example of the difference a polarizer makes. Both of these photos were of a sea anemone in a tide pool. The polarizer filter was used on the right image reducing the reflection and enhancing the color saturation.

The tide pool on the left suffers from reflections on the water. Putting a polarizer filter on the lens reduces most, if not all, the reflections, producing a better photo.

Filters like this screw on over the front lens of your camera (if your camera accepts them — not all digital cameras do). Make sure the polarizer filter you get for your camera is a circular polarizer (there are also linear polarizer filters). If it isn't, it will confuse the auto-focus capability of your camera.

Tripod

Tripods today are light and relatively inexpensive. They provide a stable platform for low-light photography and for making panoramas like the one I made using Paint Shop Photo Album's panorama feature — which I'll show you how to use in Part 5.

Travel and Care of Your Camera

A professional photographer going on a photo shoot requires a lot of gear. For general vacation photography, less is more. Here's a checklist for vacationers:

- Digital camera
- Two sets of rechargeable batteries
- Battery charger
- A fresh set of standard batteries, if your camera uses them
- Lens cleaning cloth, carry it in your pocket to keep your lens clean. (You can get a micro-cleaning cloth for about $5. They work great on eye glasses too.)
- A couple of thick, plastic sandwich bags large enough to hold your camera. Get the kind with the sliding lock. This way when you're in the snow, on water, or in rainy weather, you can keep the camera dry. Also, if you're boating on a small craft, you can keep the camera safe when it isn't in use. Put the camera in the bag and blow a little air into it (like blowing up a balloon) before sealing it. If someone accidentally drops the camera into the water it will float (unless it's a really heavy camera).

Security and Camera Bags

If you're really into photography, you may have thought about investing in a quality camera bag with all the pockets to hold your photography accessories. While these camera bags are handy, an expensive camera bag attracts thieves. For a lot of my travel, I've found a diaper bag is quite useful. It's well padded, has just as many pockets (usually more), and no self-respecting thief would look twice at a diaper bag.

Ok. That covers the digital camera basics. In Part 2 you'll discover how to use your equipment to take better photos.

Taking Better Pictures is Easy

A common complaint people have about their digital camera is that it's too complicated. In comparison to my first camera, the Kodak Flash Bantam (shown here), that's certainly true.

But while my first camera was more simplistic, taking good photos was much more complicated.

Here's what it took to capture a photo with this simple jewel:

1 Guess the distance to the subject and turn the lens to that distance setting.

2 Take a reading with a light meter (set to the correct film speed) and then make the correct shutter speed and aperture (f-stop) settings.

3 Take the photo.

4 Turn the film knob to advance the film, watching the little window for the frame number to appear so you know when to stop.

5 Wait a week (no one-hour photo places in those days) to see if the shot turned out correctly.

Even though parts of your digital camera may seem challenging, at least it makes picture taking easy. In this part of the book you'll learn some simple techniques you can use to improve your photos.

Your Digital Advantage

One of the great advantages of digital cameras is the ability to take as many photos as you want. Yet, many people continue to take photos with their digital cameras just like they do when they shoot film. If you were to make only one change in your picture taking habits, start taking more photos. Just by taking more photos you increase your chances of getting a good one. Another reason for taking lots of photos is:

Sometimes the subject blinks.

Sometimes the photo is out of focus.

Sometimes the subject blinks again.

Eventually you get the expression you were looking for. You can fix the background later.

For the record — I shot a total of ten photos that afternoon.

How Many Photos Does It Take?

National Geographic photographers are considered some of the world's finest. According to *National Geographic* magazine their photographers shoot an average of 400 rolls of film to get the photos used in one article. So:

- A typical article has 20 to 30 photos

- A roll of 35mm film has 36 exposures

- 400 x 36 = 14,400 photos

- On average they use about one out of every 500 photos — and these are some of the best photographers in the world.

Why do they shoot so many pictures? Because, when you're in the middle of the Ecuadorian jungle, you have few opportunities to go back and retake a photo.

Why should you shoot so many pictures? Because if you're in the middle of your child's fifth birthday party, a wedding, or your parents' 25th wedding anniversary, you don't have the opportunity to go back and retake the photo.

The photo to the right was taken at this couple's 25th wedding anniversary, where they renewed their vows. Their boys were acting as groomsmen, but the kissing part was too much for the youngest. I took 300 photos that afternoon and this one shot made the trip and the time worth it all.

Composition — The Secret to Great Photos

All technical matters aside, probably the most important aspect of a photo is its composition. When taking a photo you need to learn to see the entire photo, not just the subject. It only takes a second to ask yourself these two questions:

- What is the subject?

- Where is the subject within the frame?

In the top photo on the right, what would you say is the subject? I'm guessing the photographer was trying to show some attendees at a luncheon. The dominant feature in the photo is the man's back — not his best side.

Sometimes the subject is the entire scene and you just want the viewer to see what you were seeing. An example of this is the photo on the right below. It's of a fire hydrant in a small creek. There was just something delightfully absurd about a hydrant in a creek.

Rules of Composition

There are entire books written on this subject — really. On the whole, you don't need to read an entire book to understand the rules of photo composition. These rules can be distilled into three simple concepts.

- When shooting photos of people, dogs, cats, moose, or other similar subjects don't put them in the center of the photo. The exception to this guideline is passport photos — and we all know how good those look.

- When taking pictures of people it isn't necessary to get their entire body in the photo. A close-up of grandma and grandpa together showing their kindly expressions will not be made less by the fact that you didn't include all of their anatomy.

- When taking scenery shots or unusual photos you should try to put a reference point in the foreground.

Here are some examples:

In this photo I wanted to capture my son with the fall colors of Maryland as a backdrop. This is a posed photo. I had him stand so he would anchor the right third of the frame. I also told him not to look at the camera. I cut off his lower torso because it didn't add to the photo and getting closer to the subject lets the viewer see his face more clearly.

The photo (below) was taken inside a hot air balloon as it was filling. While it's a pretty shot, there's nothing to give it perspective. The photo of the balloon with the pilots lets the viewer see just how big the balloon is.

With the balloon pilots in the photo, it now becomes very apparent how large it is inside a hot air balloon.

With no reference point it's impossible to know how big or small the subject in the photograph really is.

Rules, Guidelines, and Timing

As we go through all these rules, suggestions, etc., there may be a tendency for you to begin over evaluating each photo opportunity. Don't do that, or you'll lose the moment. If you think you see a shot, take it. If the subject hasn't changed or moved, and is not charging at you (bison are not docile creatures), take another shot. If time allows, review the image you just took in the LCD screen. Then, if you need to, take another shot, and another — until you like what you get. You can always delete any unwanted duplicates and mistakes.

Make the Background Work for You — Not Against You

To a greater degree than you might imagine, you can control the background of a photo simply by changing your shooting position.

In the two bicyclist photos, the first photo has a cluttered background and the bicycle (a relatively thin machine) is pointed almost head on. Without changing my location I asked the rider to move to a different position and act as if he were getting ready to take off. The resulting photo is much less busy and the difference in angle gives the photo more energy.

Once, when several of us were taking photos, I noticed many of the photos had three or four small plastic trash cans in the background. When I asked one of the other photographers why he didn't move the trash cans, he said there was no need since we could remove them later on the computer. While this is true, it took over an hour to clone them out and clean up the photo. I figure it would have taken five minutes to move the trash cans.

You can also use background in a photo to make something in the foreground stand out. The green

tropical leaf in the background (even though it is out of focus) provides a rich backdrop for the plant in the foreground.

Consider the background when composing your shot. In this photo, the plant in the foreground is not part of the leaf in the background, but is does create an interesting composition.

Here's an easy trick for making the background appear jet-black. Change the exposure setting of your camera to Spot (check your camera's manual to see how this is done). Changing to Spot causes the camera to only read the light information at the center of the frame (usually indicated by a small rectangle near the center of the viewfinder).

Setting the exposure using the brightest part of the plant makes the background appear black.

If a subject is brightly lit (like the plant shown here), using spot metering forces the camera to adjust its exposure for the bright spot — all the other parts of the photo will be either dark or jet-black.

If the brightly-lit area is not in the center (like the example), you can point the center indicator at the bright spot and press the shutter halfway down. On just about every digital camera this will lock the exposure setting. While still holding the shutter button halfway down, recompose the shot and then press the shutter the rest of the way.

Capture the Right Amount of Light

Whether you're shooting with film or using a digital camera, controlling the amount of light that enters your camera is one of the most important factors in taking good photos. Allow too much light and the photo will be washed out (overexposed). Allow too little light and the subject gets lost in the darkened image (underexposed).

Exposure compensation can be frustrating. When you view the subject with your eye it appears to be correctly lit. The human eye is a fantastic image sensor and it can view an extremely wide range of colors and levels of light. Even the best cameras (film or digital) can only capture a fraction of that range. Subjects that contain areas of extreme highlights and shadow, like the rose shown here, look great to us but are especially tricky for cameras.

This lighting situation is challenging because it contains areas of dark shadows and bright highlights. Each area contains detail you want to capture. This demands a camera capable of capturing a wide dynamic range.

Understanding Dynamic Range

Stated simply, the dynamic range of any scene is the difference between the brightest and darkest points. Some situations, like when you're shooting on a bright sunny afternoon, can result in a larger range than the digital camera can handle. When this happens, something has to give on one end of the range; detail is either lost in the shadows or the highlights.

The photograph of an antique car on the following page was taken on a bright Texas afternoon. To capture the detail on the shadowy side of the car, the metering system was set to Spot and directed at the shadows, resulting in gross overexposure of the hood and the windshield. Areas of an image that go completely white are called blowouts.

Tip

In most cases adjusting your exposure to get detail in shadows results in blowouts in the bright (highlight) region.

Overexposure with digital cameras can be a little more problematic than with film, because film has a relatively large tolerance with overexposure. The same overexposure with a digital camera sensor produces sharp cutoffs that appear as areas of solid white in the photo. Unfortunately, there's no way to recover the detail from a blowout.

There are, however, several techniques that help prevent blowouts.

Expose for the Bright Spots and Hope for the Best

Expose for the highlights and adjust for the shadows is a standard axiom of photography (both film and digital). By using spot metering you can measure the brightest spot in the scene. This prevents any loss of detail in the highlight region, but it can also make the resulting image quite dark.

The photo shown on the right was taken on a sunny morning. The red leaves were brightly lit, so they were measured with the camera's meter set to Spot. The background appears much darker than it looked when I took the photo. In this situation, the darker background provides a good backdrop for the red leaves. Even though some detail might be lost in the shadows, it wasn't necessary for the overall composition of this photo.

Using Exposure Value Settings

Another way to compensate for scenes with wide dynamic range is accomplished by using the camera's Exposure Value (EV) compensation (sometimes known simply as Exposure Compensation). Many digital cameras offer the option to adjust EV. You might have to dig out the manual to find out how to do this. EV adjust is a handy feature that lets you override the auto exposure system and lighten or darken an image. The information in the shadow regions of a slightly underexposed image can be recovered later in Paint Shop Pro or Paint Shop Photo Album. While underexposing an image can prevent blowouts, you must also be careful not to underexpose the image so much that you can't recover the important details in the shadow.

If the photo you're taking is really important, you can try shooting like the professionals. Shoot the same scene using different exposure settings. Most mid- to high-end cameras offer the ability to Auto Bracket the exposure settings. How it works and what operational features are available differ between cameras, but overall it works like this: when Auto Bracket is enabled, each time the shutter is pressed, a series of three to five shots is taken in quick succession with each photo taken at a different exposure setting. Back home, you can evaluate and select the photo with the best exposure.

Capturing the Action — Tips for Taking Action Shots

Thanks to the billions of dollars spent every year on sports advertising, we've become accustomed to seeing some incredible photographs of athletes captured in some equally incredible action poses. It's been said that you cannot shoot action with a digital camera. That's not true, as this photo of a young man bursting a water balloon on his dad shows.

The first time you attempt to capture an action scene with your digital camera you may discover a feature that's not described in the camera's brochure. I'm speaking about shutter delay – the delay that occurs from the time that you push the shutter button until the time your camera finally gets around to taking the photo.

What is Shutter Delay?

With your basic film camera, there is no delay. You press the shutter all the way down; you take a picture — that's it. But with most digital cameras when you press the shutter, the camera doesn't take the picture. Why? Because each time you press the shutter button, you start a long sequence of events inside your camera.

Assuming your camera is on, the image sensor in the camera must be cleared so it can begin receiving the image information reflected by the subject. Depending on the settings, your camera may try to focus (which can take a long time) before it takes the picture.

These processes take time. Depending on the make and model of your camera, the delay between the moment you press the shutter and the time the camera actually captures the image can be anything from a barely noticeable lag up to a full second or more. A second may not seem like much time, but when taking action photos, it's the difference between catching the action and a photo with no one in it.

Compensating for Shutter Delay

It is possible to capture action with your digital camera with a little preparation and exercise, despite the shutter delay. There are several things you can do to be prepared for the photo. These preparations will lessen the effect of the shutter's delay.

- **Make sure your camera is on** – Many people leave their camera off to save their batteries. Most digital cameras will go into a standby mode to conserve battery power after a few minutes of inactivity. So, before taking the shot, make sure your camera is on. If it's in standby, either push the shutter or turn it off and on again to wake it up.

- **Pre-focus your camera** – Another feature that eats up time is the auto-focus. When you focus on any subject, the camera reads the contrast of the scene to determine when the scene is in focus. This can take anywhere from one-half to two seconds, depending on your camera.

  When preparing to shoot an action shot, you can pre-focus by pressing the shutter halfway down. This will cause the camera to focus and set the exposure settings. When you are ready to take the photo, just push the shutter the rest of the way down.

- **Practice Shots** – Practice taking action shots using a moving subject – like someone on a swing. Your goal is to catch the person at the top of the swing.

  On the average, it will take you about twenty minutes before you can consistently capture the person on the swing every time. Once you start capturing the swinger consistently, you'll have developed a learned response. From now on when you take action shots, you'll know when to push the shutter in order to capture the action.

Catching the Action

After you've prepared, I suggest that you shoot lots and lots of action photos. If you have the time, review the shot after you take it and delete it (especially if it's an empty frame).

Here are suggestions that apply to both film and digital cameras.

- **Pan the camera** - If the action is moving by you — like a race — you should move your camera with the action. As the person, horse, or car is moving by, move the camera along with them as you take the photo. This is called panning a shot and it helps keep the subject in the camera's field of view.

- **Pull in that zoom lens** - Use as wide a lens setting as reasonable. The more you zoom in on a subject, the narrower the field of view. This makes it more difficult to capture your subject. Better to have extra to crop than to have an empty frame.

- **Move around** - Experiment with different locations. Move yourself around the action you're trying to capture. Some positions are better than others and this is something that's difficult to figure out just by thinking it through. You'll be amazed by how much difference your shooting location can make.

Here's the best of roughly 40 images I shot within a 10 minute span. These kids were instructed to catch the orange water balloons with their shirts – which explains what the boys on the left and right were attempting. The rest were going to catch the water balloon any way they could. Maybe they'd have succeeded if they had opened their eyes!

While water balloon catching might not be the stuff of great sports photography, it's a lot of fun for the photographer and the balloon catcher.

White Balance and Your Camera Settings

The transition from film to digital is relatively painless since digital cameras on the whole look and act so much like their film counterparts. One area unique to digital photography is how color is controlled.

It's hard to recognize how different types (temperatures) of lighting affect our photos, since our brain instantly corrects for this. But the color of incandescent lighting (regular light bulbs), fluorescent lighting, sunlight, and overcast skies are dramatically different. Unless this is compensated for, the resulting photos appear to have an overall color shift, or "cast", that can look unnatural.

In conventional photography you can compensate for these different lighting situations using different film types or color correction filters. For the digital photographer, the camera corrects color temperature. Called white balance, it's a new concept for most conventional photographers, although videographers have always worked with it. Without getting too technical, white balance controls what a digital camera perceives as true white. Without white balance correction, white objects tend

A bluish color cast is a common problem seen in photos taken in bright sunlight.

to appear yellowish-white under incandescent lights, slightly green under fluorescent lights, or bluish on an overcast day.

Adjusting the white balance for a sunny day results in warmer, more accurate colors.

The Alamo photo above was taken on a bright, sunny day with the incorrect white-balance setting, resulting in a photo with a bluish overcast. The photo on the left was taken moments later with the correct white-balance settings.

To understand why white balance works the way it does, it would help to understand some of the basics of color temperature. Even though the light from the sun or a light bulb looks white to us, it contains a mixture of all the colors in varying proportions. Color temperature describes the color of a light source. The color temperature scale is calibrated in degrees Kelvin, much like a thermometer reads heat in degrees Fahrenheit. The color temperature scale operates opposite from what might be expected. That is, the lower color temperatures (reddish light) are called warmer and the high color temperatures (bluish light) are cooler. For example, daylight contains proportionately more light at the blue end of the spectrum while incandescent light is made up of light at the red end. Hence daylight photos appear "cooler" and candlelight shots appear "warmer." I've listed a few of the more common color temperatures from different sources.

- 1500K Candlelight (very warm or reddish)
- 2700K Incandescent lamp (still quite red)
- 3400 – 4000K Within one hour of dawn or dusk
- 5000 – 5500K Mid-morning or mid-afternoon
- 5200 – 5600K Sunlight at noon (near neutral)
- 6000 – 7500K Heavy overcast skies (cool or bluish)

Automatic White Balance

Digital cameras have an automatic white balance (AWB) feature that would, at face value, solve all color balance problems. In the real world however, even the best AWB mechanisms can be fooled by lighting conditions or color content of the subject matter being photographed. Images with a dominant color, such as large areas of blue sky and green grass, may cause the AWB on some digital cameras to produce an incorrect white point that gives the photo a color cast.

Many cameras include white-balance presets for daylight, cloudy, incandescent, and fluorescent light that work well most of the time. But you should be aware that the white-balance presets are not infallible and the AWB might produce an inaccurate color reading. It's best to experiment with the presets and familiarize yourself with your camera's lighting sweet spot. Even though the LCD preview of your camera isn't the most accurate color device, you can use it to compare several images of the same subject taken with different presets. On the LCD it's possible to see the lighting differences and choose the setting that produces the best results.

White Balance Calibration

Professional digital cameras and some mid-range models include a white-balance preset that allows for the calibration of the white balance. You set the white point by pointing the camera at a white or gray object. When using this method to set the white-balance, it's important to remember to reset your white-balance or return the camera to the AWB setting when you're done shooting or the lighting changes.

If your camera offers the ability to set your white point, add a piece of white paper to your camera bag. It takes only a moment to set the camera for a white-balance preset. Just shoot the white paper and you'll get an accurate white balance.

You can intentionally set an incorrect white balance to create the effect of a colored filter. For example, if you set the white balance using a colored card, your images will have a color cast that is the opposite of the card's color. An excellent product for this is a set of colored cards called Warm Cards from Vortex media (www.warmcards.com).

Another consideration when working with color balance doesn't involve capturing accurate color as much as getting the color you desire. The photograph below on the left was taken with the white-balance accurately adjusted. The colors in the photograph are accurate, but not so appealing.

The photo on the right is the same pier photographed using a cloudy white-balance preset. This produced a much cooler image that better fit the mood of the early morning at low tide.

While the colors in this photo are technically accurate, they don't set the correct mood.

By deliberately setting the white balance incorrectly, I was able to give this low tide photo a cool bluish tone.

Part 3

Organizing and Safeguarding Your Photos

Taking pictures has traditionally been a three-part operation. After taking the photos, you had to get the film processed and printed, then it's time to then organize and display the photos. Like many people, I had the first two parts down to a science. The third part has always been my downfall, as several large storage boxes full of photographs will attest.

Let's face it; if you're really creative, you're inherently disorganized. I don't know if that last statement is really true, but I read it once in an ad for image management software and thought it sounded good. The best part is, if it's true, I may be one of the most creative people on the planet. In earlier parts of this book you learned about digital cameras and ways to improve your photography. Now we're going to tackle what happens after you capture the shot or, as this section could be called, *"What do I do with all of these photos and where is the one I'm looking for?"*

Getting Photos Out of Your Camera and Into Your Computer

This topic is covered in great detail in both the Paint Shop Pro and Paint Shop Photo Album User Guides, as well as in my book, *How to Do Everything with Paint Shop Pro 8*. So I'm just going to give a few tips on the fastest ways to move images from your digital camera to your computer.

Most digital cameras today come with a USB cable that attaches to the computer and is used to transfer photos. In most cases this works well. But if you don't leave your USB camera cable connected to your computer, or if it seems to take too much time to download images, there's a faster way to move those photos.

If you use a card reader, either a PCMCIA card (also called a PC card) adapter or a card reader that attaches to the USB port, you'll discover you can download images faster. Plus, using a reader has an added advantage in that your camera doesn't need to be powered on (running down its batteries). The card reader shown is a six-way reader that attaches to a USB port. If you're going to get a card reader, the advantage of a six-way is that not only can it read the media from your camera, but it can also read different types of media. You can get photos from friends and family, right from their media card.

So, were you wondering how a card reader attached to a USB port could be any faster than hooking up your camera to the same USB port? Good for you. The download speed using the camera's USB feature is managed by the camera itself, wherein the card reader is controlled directly by the computer so there's no middleman to slow things down. For notebook computer users, there's the added advantage of the PCMCIA card readers in that they use the PC card slot and don't take up one of the limited number of USB ports.

Tip

USB 2.0 devices (cameras, scanners, card readers) will work on USB 1.0/1.1 ports — they just won't transfer data at USB 2.0 speeds.

Card readers today are inexpensive and there's little to no difference between the least expensive and the most expensive ones. While I wouldn't label a card reader as a necessary accessory for a digital camera, I do consider it an important one.

Using Paint Shop Photo Album to Import Photos

Whether you're using the camera's built-in USB connection or a card reader, when you plug into the computer things start to happen. If your operating system is Windows XP (either Home or Professional) a dialog will pop up (like the one shown) asking you to select the application you'd like to use to download images. Depending on the number of image applications installed on your computer, you could be presented with a list like the one shown on the right.

You have the option to always have Windows open Paint Shop Photo Album whenever the camera or a card reader is attached by marking the **Always do the selected action** box. As a rule, I do not recommend checking it. This way you always have the option of selecting what action is taken when an external device is attached.

At this point, select Paint Shop Photo Album and click **OK**. This will launch Photo Album and the images on either the camera or card reader appear in the Album view as a filmstrip (shown on the left).

To copy all the images from the camera into an album (which is what a Windows folder is called), click the **Get All** button. All the images on the camera or media will be selected and another dialog appears asking you to name a new album for the images.

Albums, Folders, and Other Things

If all the photos in the camera are from a single time (a vacation, Christmas) or event (a birthday, a wedding), put them in the same album. By default Photo Album will name the folder with today's date. If you're using Photo Album for all your image management, there's no need to include the date as part of the album name since Photo Album can search for images by date. By clicking the **Browse** button you can change the default location where the images will be stored. After you click **OK**, the images will be copied to the new album.

If your camera's media card contains photos from many different events, Photo Album gives you the option to download a single image or a selected set of images, each to its own album. In cases where the photos are not event oriented (sunsets, wildflowers, rivers) you should create an album for each subject, then select and download the photos into their respective, aptly named albums.

Remember, it's OK to have an album with only one or two photos in it. As time moves on, the contents will increase.

Sorting Your Photos

After loading the photos into an album, your next step should be to review the photos. This serves several purposes. It lets you remove the throwaways (thumb over lens, out of focus, etc.) and rotate the photos so they're in the correct orientation.

Using Photo Album, here's how it's done:

1 Select the album containing the photos you want to review.

2 Click the **Slide Show** button.

3 As soon as the show begins, click the **Stop** button in the Slide Show control bar, shown in the next photo.

Single steps   Rotate image   Select image

4 Using the step buttons, advance from one photo to the next. If the photo in the slide is sideways, use the rotate buttons to correct the orientation. For photos you don't want to keep, click the Select Image button. This selects the image and doesn't delete it.

5 When the slide show is finished, Photo Album displays the thumbnails with the images you selected during the slide show highlighted. Pressing the **Del** key will send these images to the Recycle Bin.

6 At this point you have corrected the orientation of all the photos in the Album and you have deleted the bad photos — erasing any evidence of their existence.

What is a Bad Photo?

When it comes to getting rid of bad photos, there are several schools of thought.

- Keep them all – even the bad ones.

- Keep only the very best – even if you have three outstanding photos of the same subject taken from slightly different angles or settings keep only the best one and delete the rest.

- Mark the best as keepers using a keyword (more on that in the next section) and only throw away the really bad ones.

Even with Photo Album, keeping everything you shoot just clutters up your drive and doesn't serve any good purpose. The *only the very best* philosophy works to keep your collection to a minimum size, and forces you to throw away photos that, for one reason or another, you may want at a later date. The third alternative – keeping all acceptable photos and marking the exceptional ones with keywords preserves the better part of your collection. Plus, with this method, you can perform a simple keyword search and present an excellent photographic representation of an event.

Tip

There will be some photos of individuals or events that may be photographically imperfect. Don't forget that their value is not in their perfection but in capturing a moment in time. Don't delete those photos.

Using Keywords

After you've placed your photos in an album, you should assign keywords. If you don't assign keywords, you won't be able to use one of the best features of Photo Album – the ability to perform custom searches on those keywords. For example, you could search for images that include your daughter and her cat; or you could see all the photos of your trip to Hawaii.

If working with keywords is new to you, here are some suggestions for what and what not to do.

Avoid keyword overkill. That is, don't assign keywords for everything in the photo. If you carefully examine almost any photo you can find a lot of objects in it that could be assigned keywords. Before you begin assigning keywords, you have to ask yourself, "When I want to find this photo later, what words will I associate with it?"

For example – the following photo was taken at a tea house in the Seisui Tea Garden at the Arboretum operated by the University of Minnesota in Minneapolis.

I could assign the following keywords:

- Seisui
- Garden
- Tea
- Water
- Pipe
- Stone
- Bamboo
- Ladle
- Minnesota
- University
- Minneapolis
- Arboretum
- Japanese pine (plant in the back-ground)

Assigning keywords for all 13 items would be a little over the top.

Keywords that Work

Keywords work best when they're generic. Remember that when you do a keyword search, you're not trying to select the individual image as much as you are trying to get in the ballpark. This way you only have to visually browse through a small number of photos that have matching keywords to find the right one, and not your entire photo collection.

What keywords work best is a very individual decision.

Here are the keywords I assigned for the tea garden photo above:

- Minnesota
- Minneapolis
- Oriental
- Garden
- Arboretum

When I'm looking for a photo, I generally remember where I shot it, so I always assign locations (city and state) to every image. Point in fact, the Arboretum is not located in Minneapolis but in a city near it. The odds are I won't remember the name of the city when I go to search, so I usually label my photos with the name of the nearest big city and lump all of the surrounding areas together.

Keeping Track of Where You've Been

I would probably remember the Arboretum but even if I didn't, it's on the keyword list and I can quickly develop a list of all of the photos I took there — and I took a lot.

Although this was located in the Seisui Tea Garden, there were only two photos taken in the garden; therefore I wouldn't create a keyword that would not have many other photos attached to it. The name wouldn't be lost, since it can be put in either the photo's title or description. But this brings up another important topic. Being as I have a very poor memory for names, how did I remember the name *Seisui Tea Garden* to include in the title?

Of course, you could jot them down on a small note pad (but I always lose the note pads). Here are my tried and true ways to keep track of the names of places: in the case of the Seisui Tea Garden, I had picked up one of the free brochures/maps for the Arboretum which named all the locations I shot that day. That evening when I imported my photos, I added the appropriate information to the titles and descriptions.

The other way is to take a picture of the signage (if there is any). In this regard, your digital camera becomes a great note taker and the pictures can also come in handy when making a slide show. Here are a few examples of the hundreds of signs I've photographed (yes, I do keep them).

Of course, some photos provide their own description. This is a photo of an office – in case you were wondering.

Creating and Assigning Keywords

Photo Album's User Guide gives detailed step-by-step instructions on how this is done.

Here's my version in a nutshell:

1 With an album open, click the **Keywords** tab on the left. If this is the first time you've done this, you'll see a small set of categories that Jasc provided. As I mentioned earlier, the first keyword should be the location where the images were taken (assuming they were all shot at the same location). Looking at the image below, it's pretty clear where they were taken. You were going to say Houston, Texas, right? Actually it's located in Katy, Texas (home of Renée Zellweger). As you learned earlier, it's usually easier to assign keyword locations of the nearest big city. Looking again at the photo – there isn't a keyword named Houston. So we need to add one.

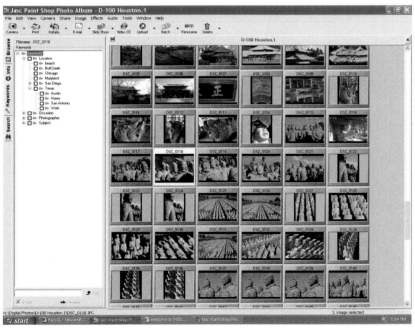

2 Clicking on the word Texas (which I added to the location list immediately after installing Photo Album), I type the word Houston in the small text box at the bottom and click **Add**. Now Houston appears as a keyword under Texas.

3 To assign the keyword Houston to all the images in the album, select all the photos by pressing **Ctrl+A**, this will highlight all the photos. Mark the box next to the keyword Houston. That's all there is to it.

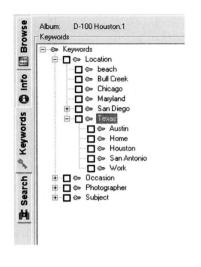

Search Using Keywords

Finding photos based on a keyword search is easy. Click the **Search** tab, make sure **Search by: Keywords** is selected, mark the box in front of the keyword you want to search by, and click **Search**. An album labeled Search Results opens and displays thumbnails of all of the images matching the selected keyword.

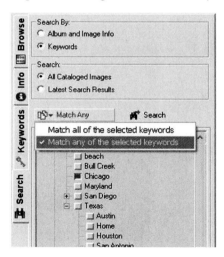

You can search on multiple keywords and, depending on the search criteria setting, the search results window will only display the images that match some or all of the selected keywords. **Match Any** will show a larger set of photos containing at least one of the selected keywords. **Match All** will show a smaller set of only the photos containing all of the selected keywords.

Safeguarding Your Images

In Photo Album, Jasc has included the ability to protect your images from change or accidental deletion. Once you have finished working on an album, you can lock the images. From the Album View window, right-click an image or images, choose **Lock** from the context menu. The locked image will be protected from changes or deletion until you un-lock the image by right-clicking the image and selecting **Un-lock** from the context menu.

Archiving Your Images

The good news, digital photos cannot be scratched, stained, torn, or bent. They also cannot fade over time or become brittle. That's the good news. The bad news, digital photos can disappear. If the hard drive on your computer fails this afternoon all of the photos you have stored on it will be lost. That means if you have three years of family photos and a virus wipes out your hard drive, all of the photos are gone and, in some cases, cannot be recovered. How important are those photos to you?

I have taken photos in the aftermath of both floods and tornados (we get the best of all worlds in Texas). As I talk to the victims who are looking at the pile of debris that was once their home, the item they usually mention first when describing what they lost is family photos.

Backing Up Your Photos – Make it a Habit

Sobering thought isn't it? I bring this up, not to give you sleepless nights worrying about your photos, but to prove a point. Truth be known, worrying about things works. I find that 95 percent of the things I worry about never happen. Regarding the hard drive on your computer, I worked in the hard drive industry when they were fragile, short-lived devices. Today's drives are statistically approaching fail-proof. Still, you need to develop a plan and make it a habit to safeguard these very important documents. It isn't hard, and doesn't cost much so here's what you need to do.

- **Decide where you'll back-up your photos** – There are a lot of options today. The most popular choice is to burn copies of the photos to CD. Even if your computer doesn't have a CD burner, you can buy an external burner for under $100. Blank CDs are sold in spindle packs of 100 for under $20. Each CD can hold 700MB, which translates to a lot of saved photos. Now that DVD-burners are becoming reasonably priced, this is a viable option. DVDs offer more than 4GB of storage per disc, and the cost of blank DVDs is dropping every day. The other choice you have is to buy a second hard drive and create a duplicate set of photos.

- **Decide how and when you will back-up your photos** – There are two general approaches to back-up: backing up by event and backing up by schedule. Event back-up means that each time you attend an event where you take a lot of photos (wedding, birthday, moose migrations) you burn a CD containing all the images from the shoot. The disadvantage of this approach is that it's an inefficient use of CDs. While you can add more photos to a CD after you've burned it (if you leave the session open) you typically end up with a lot of unused storage space. Since I'm paying roughly 15¢ per CD, it's not an issue for me. If you do a traditional weekly back-up then the back-up software (Did you know Windows has built-in backup software?) will put the maximum number of photos on each CD.

- **Label and catalog your back-up media** – Sounds really simple right? Many people forget this important step and then, when they need to find the CD containing the award-winning moose migration photo, they have to load, read, and unload dozens of CDs to find the right one. Photo Album has a feature that lets you make a Video CD. By checking a box in the initial set-up dialog, Photo Album will copy the original files to the CD along with the Video CD slide show. After the photos are copied to CD use Photo Album's catalog command to catalog the CD. Now, Photo Album knows where the photos are. Next time you search for the photos, Photo Album will be able to tell you which CD contains the photo you're looking for. Photo Album can search all your cataloged CDs, they don't have to be in the computer while you're searching.

Urban Myth

Silver CD-Rs are not as reliable for long-term storage as gold CDs. This is not true. Both have the same 100-year life expectancy.

Do CDs Last Forever?

Most people are surprised when they're told that CDs will fade after a period of time – usually quoted as 25 years. Let's take a moment and put that rumor to rest. According to four of the leading blank CD manufacturers, under proper storage conditions (read: don't store in car trunk in Dallas during July), you can expect photos you've put onto CD to last 100 years. But in the age of emerging technologies, one must ponder if the hardware/software necessary to read the CD will be available in even 50 years. Hence, you or your grandkids may have to transfer data to a newer medium for true archiving.

Part 4

Working with Non-Digital Images

Up to now we've only considered working with a digital camera to take your photos. We're surrounded with non-digital memorabilia of people, places, and events that are the touchstones of our daily life. These physical souvenirs of our life's journey take many forms: tickets to events, dog tags, dried flowers, a diploma, newspaper clippings, and more than a thousand other non-digital reminders of our past. This desire to organize, collect, and display what we have done in our lives has led to the rising popularity of creating scrapbooks. These books chronicle the events that make up our lives and the lives of those around us. The scrapbook pages shown represent only a few of the thousands of scrapbooks that have been and are being created everyday.

This part of the book is about how to use your scanner as a sort of digital camera to capture all sorts of materials, and then how to use Paint Shop Pro to make these new digital images into keepsakes that will last a lifetime.

Paint Shop Pro and Your Scanner

I'm going to assume you have a scanner that's properly installed. I'm also assuming everything works so we can spend our time learning how to do cool stuff. If you want to learn all about scanners and what can be done with them, may I be so bold as to recommend my book *How to Do Everything with Your Scanner*? If you buy and read this book you'll learn a lot about scanners and, more importantly, my daughter is getting married next year and I would appreciate the royalties.

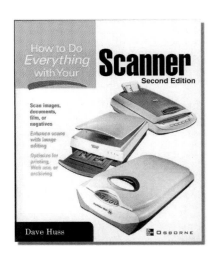

The Power of Scanned Images

Let's jump right into a simple scan project and we'll cover a couple of scanning basics while we do it. At the moment we're having a heat wave where I live. Mark Twain said it best, "Everybody talks about the weather but nobody does anything about it." The e-mail traffic to friends and alike has been peppered with talk about the record-breaking heat. An e-mail like the one shown next can describe the current weather in accurate detail.

Although it is accurate and conveys the facts, it doesn't have the visual impact created by embedding a few headlines from the local papers.

E-mails are textual and factual, but generally don't get much attention. By scanning the headlines from the local paper it's possible to convey the impact of our local heat wave.

Capturing and Sharing Newsprint

In this project we'll be covering several topics; the first, how to scan material printed on newsprint. Newsprint needs to be scanned because it has a short shelf life. The grade of paper called newsprint is designed to carry daily news, wrap garbage, and line the bottom of birdcages. Longevity is not required. When you use your scanner to make an electronic copy of a newspaper column about some important event, you have halted the aging process and regardless of what fate befalls the original, you have captured the information in a form that will not fade.

The Dick Van Dyke Show wasn't in Black and White

In the world of computer graphics, black and white and grayscale are different. When we say something is black and white (also called line art), we're describing an image made of tiny black and white squares (pixels). Grayscale images are made of pixels that can be any one of 256 shades of gray from black to white. So, all of those TV shows from the 1950s were actually in grayscale, not black and white. Technically, your black and white photos are also grayscale. Outside of image editing, black and white and grayscale are generally accepted as the same thing. Just remember that in Paint Shop Pro, they are two different formats.

The Challenges of Scanning Newsprint

Newsprint can be challenging to scan because it's generally very thin. When you scan newsprint you can often see what's printed on the other side, like the scan shown below of a real news tidbit that appeared in this morning's paper. The appearance of what is printed on the other side is called bleed-through. The image on the left was scanned using a 24-bit color setting (using a grayscale setting produces the same results) while the image on the right was scanned as a black and white image (see *The Dick Van Dyke Show wasn't in Black and White*).

'Hello, Sexy, how are you? You're supposed to talk to your plants, right?'

Ricky Martin
Singer, speaking to a Renaglottis Ricky Martin, a hybrid orchid named after him by the Singapore Tourism Board.

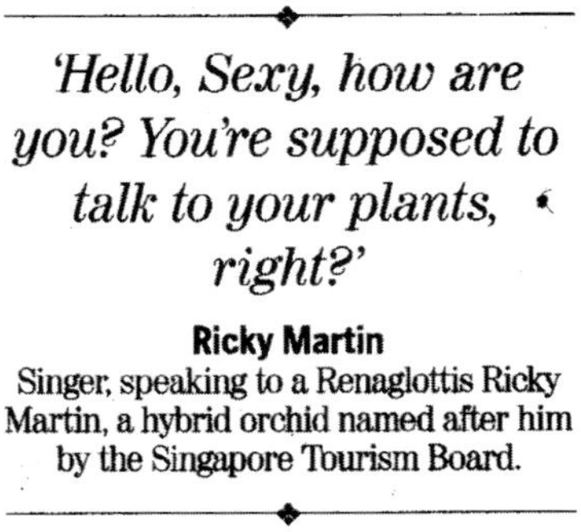

'Hello, Sexy, how are you? You're supposed to talk to your plants, right?'

Ricky Martin
Singer, speaking to a Renaglottis Ricky Martin, a hybrid orchid named after him by the Singapore Tourism Board.

Scanning thin paper like newsprint can reveal bleed-through as seen on the left. But scanning as Black and White may reveal excessive anti-aliasing.

While it appears that scanning text as black and white (also called 1-bit or line art) is the solution, there are several limitations to this format. First and most important, any image that is composed only of black and white pixels cannot be resized without suffering greatly in overall appearance. The second issue with scanning as line art is that most of the tools and filters in Paint Shop Pro and Paint Shop Photo Album will not work on 1-bit images.

Preventing Bleed-Through on Thin Paper

Here are two tried and true techniques to prevent your scanner from seeing through to the other side of the media you're scanning.

- **Put a piece of black paper behind the material you're scanning**. Trust me, having a dark background behind the paper greatly reduces bleed through. If you don't have a sheet of black construction paper handy, almost anything dark will do. At work the other day I only had a black notebook. I lifted the lid and put it over the paper I was scanning and it did the trick.

Adjusting the exposure manually is another way to avoid bleed-through and get a clean scan.

- **Manually adjust the exposure adjustment settings**. The automatic exposure mechanism of your scanner always tries to set the scanner controls so it can capture as much detail as possible. In other words, it's trying to capture the information printed on the other side of the paper. In the adjoining screen capture, I've shown our news blurb along with the Adjustment dialog of one of my HP scanners. Every scanner I have worked with has a manual exposure override. Don't let the sliders and buttons spook you. After making sure your scanner is set to grayscale mode (if you're scanning text on newsprint) just move the sliders until the black is as black as possible without the material on the other side appearing.

How to Get Great Scans Consistently

If you follow these suggestions you can ensure you get the best scans your scanner has to offer:

- **Clean the copy glass of your scanner – often**. If you don't, you'll end up with debris on the photograph or whatever else you're scanning. You can remove the debris using Paint Shop Pro's Clone brush, but you'd save time by just cleaning the glass. See *Cleaning Your Scanner Glass*.

- **Keep your copy straight on the scanner glass** – Paint Shop Pro has a great tool that will straighten a crooked scan, instantly. As good as the Straighten tool is, anytime you rotate a digital image it degrades slightly. So, to get the best scan possible, take a little extra time and ensure whatever you are scanning is lined up correctly on the glass. In the next section, I will show you some tips on how to achieve a straight scan.

- **Verify the color mode the scanner is using** – Today's scanning software is pretty darn smart, but sometimes the automatic tools get it wrong. Specifically, if they think you're scanning something for use on the Web, it assumes (incorrectly) that you want to make a copy of the image in 8-bit (also called 256-color) mode.

Scan all non-color images using grayscale and all color images at the highest color setting the scanner supports. This color mode is called by many names. Here are a few that I'm aware of:

- 24-bit color

- 16.7 million colors

- Millions of colors (popular with HP scanners)

- True color (do not confuse with High Color which is another name for 16-bit color)

- 32-bit color

- RGB-color

Cleaning Your Scanner Glass

The only hope you have of always cleaning your scanner glass is to keep a small bottle of glass cleaner and wipes near the scanner. Just spray the cloth (never directly spray the scanner copy glass) and wipe the glass. A good way to evaluate how well you cleaned the glass is to lift the lid and, with nothing on the glass, initiate a scan. As the recording head lights up you'll see everything you missed on the glass.

Be aware that some copy glass may appear to be slightly fogged on the underside. This is normal and you shouldn't try to remove the glass to clean it, unless the manufacturer has provided specific instructions on how to do this. I've only seen one scanner manufacturer that did, and they're out of business.

Similar to Line Art or Black and White mode, you don't want to use 8-bit color because some of the filters and tools in Paint Shop Pro and Paint Shop Photo Album will not work on 8-bit images. The other reason is that if you need to resize the image, the colors will degrade and become . . . ugly.

The example shown on the left was scanned at 24-bit color and then resized to 300 percent of the original size. The same photo on the right was scanned as an 8-bit color (256-color) image and was also resized to 300 percent. Any questions?

Avoid scanning photos as 256-colors (8-bit) because when the photo is resized, it can often break apart very badly as shown on the right.

Creating a Straight Scan

A classic way to ensure an image is straight is to line up the edge of the photo with the edge of the scanner glass. In a pinch this will work, but as a general rule, if a scanner has a weak area, it's along the edges of the scanner glass. I recommend that you add a plastic triangle to your collection of graphic art tools.

Tip

After placing any image on the scanner glass, be careful when closing the scanner lid. This will prevent the air whoosh that likes to move things around.

Place the triangle against the edge and then use the straight edge to align the photo, like the one shown. Normally, only the photo would be seen in the scan, I included the triangle for demonstration.

Scanning Little Photos

If you own a scanner, at sometime or another you'll be faced with the formidable task of scanning one of those itty-bitty little photos that schools seem to create in vast quantities. (See the *Scanning, Copyrights and the Law* section at the end of Part 4.) The problem with these photos is they're all printed together on a single 8 x 10 sheet. So, when they're cut up to give to friends and relatives the edges of the photos are often crooked.

Here's how to scan any small photo:

1 Clean the photo with a soft brush.

2 Use a pad of quadrille or graph paper and a glue stick of restickable adhesive (this is the same type of adhesive used on Post-It™ notes) and put a little on the paper.

3 Use a clear straight edge (like the plastic triangle) to position the photo so the edge of the actual image (not the edge of the photograph's paper) is aligned with one of the grid lines on the paper as shown.

4 Press the photo on the paper and then place it face down on the scanner, aligning the edge of the paper with the edge of the glass. It's OK to use the edge since the actual photo is nowhere near the edge.

Resizing with Your Scanner

The little photo shown above is only 1½ x 2 ¼ inches but I want to make a larger photo to frame. Paint Shop Pro can resize this photo to any size I want. But, as with all image editors, when you enlarge a digital image the quality may suffer. To enlarge an image, the existing pixels must appear larger (this means the image will have a lower resolution) or additional pixels must be added (called interpolation). Either way, the overall quality of the image degrades. How much depends on how large you're making the image.

This following example shows a photo scanned from a school yearbook that was enlarged 400 percent using Paint Shop Pro's Resize command. The photo on the right was also increased by 400 percent, this time using the scanner. There is nothing wrong with the resize command, this is the kind of degradation seen whenever a low-quality image is resized.

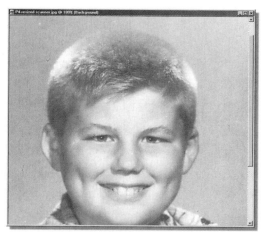

Thankfully, there's a better way to enlarge an image – your scanner. The next photo shows the resize dialog for the scanning software of the scanner I was using. By changing the output to a larger size, the scanner will scan the photo at a high enough resolution so that the finished image is almost 5 x 7 inches. By using the scanner to make the scanned photos larger (called scaling), the overall quality of the finished photo is notice-ably better.

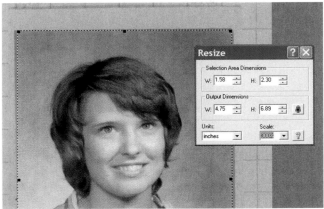

Your scanning software should contain controls (shown above) for resizing a scanned image.

Later we'll discover how to restore old photos and make them into glamour shots like the one shown below. On the left is the original scanned 1½ x 2¼-inch photo and on the right the restored 4 x 6-inch photo. Scanners are not magic photo fixers — if the small original image isn't in good shape, the enlarged original won't look any better. But you can fix some of that with Paint Shop Pro. The advantage the scanner offers is the ability to enlarge without making the image worse.

Scanning Negatives and Color Slides

Many scanners today come equipped with options that allow you to scan negatives and color slides (also called positives).

If you have a small number of negatives or slides, you can get satisfactory results from the transparency adapters on many scanners made in the past few years (the scanner resolution must be at least 1200 dpi). If you have a large number of negatives or slides, I recommend the purchase of a dedicated film scanner.

These scanners used to be expensive ($2,000 - $4,000) but today you can get a professional quality film scanner for less than $500. If you choose to buy one, get a scanner that offers a feature called Digital ICE. This feature does such a good job of removing scratches, dirt, and other debris that the first time I saw it demonstrated I accused the person doing the demo of doctoring the results. There are at least six manufacturers that offer film scanners with Digital ICE.

Scanning Objects Larger Than Your Scanner

Most scanners today can scan images up to 8 ½ x 12 inches. More expensive scanners can accommodate legal sized documents. These scanners can scan an area a little larger than 8 ½ x 14 inches. If you use your scanner to capture older documents, you'll discover there are lots of things larger than your scanner. The two classic examples are:

- Scrapbook pages
- Old panorama class photos

Scanning objects larger than your scanner is relatively simple. A classic example of this is scanning in a 12 x 12 inch scrapbook page.

Here's how to do it:

1 Scan in each half of the page. Since the scrapbook page is 12 inches wide and the scanner is typically 9 inches wide, there will be a lot of overlap, as appears in the two halves of the scanned pages shown below.

2 Open one of the scanned pages in Paint Shop Pro, and using the Canvas size command, make the image about 12 ½ inches wide.

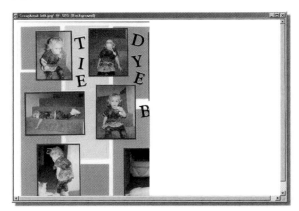

3 Open the second image and copy the image to the Windows Clipboard. Select All (**Ctrl+A**) and Copy to Clipboard (**Ctrl+C**).

4 Close the second image and don't save the changes.

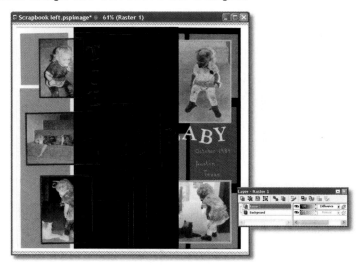

5 With the original expanded image selected, paste the contents of the clipboard as a new Layer (**Ctrl+L**). In the Layer palette change the Blend mode to Difference. Now you can see through the page you just added. Select the Move tool and move the layer so it aligns with the layer below it as shown.

6 When the two pages are aligned, change the Blend mode back to Normal and then use the Eraser tool with a soft edge (Hardness 25) to remove the edge of the layer. What you're doing here is removing the dark edge of the top scanned image. Because of the large amount of overlap, any of the top layer that is removed reveals the bottom layer.

7 After the edge is gone, flatten the image (**Layers > Merge > Merge All**) and the scanned parts are stitched together. You have succeeded in scanning a 12 x 12 inch image with a scanner that is only 9 inches wide.

Paint Shop Photo Album has a wonderful panorama feature. Photo Album's panorama feature was designed to stitch together digital photos, and it attempts to correct for non-existent barrel distortion.

Tip

There are scanners that can scan an entire scrapbook page. They are called tabloid or oversize scanners and their scanning area is 11 x 17 inches.

Repairing the Effects of Time

Next, we'll look at how to restore faded color photos since the dyes in many color photos dating from the 60s and 70s are beginning to show the effects of age. The colors are slowly changing and the detail is getting soft. The photo that I'm working with in this section is of my niece, Patty. I'm not sure when this photo was taken but she's now a grandmother (five times). The original was one of those little school photos 1½ by 2¼ inches. Unlike many framed photos, this one was kept in a photo album so it wasn't exposed to fading caused by sunlight. Let's go through the procedure step-by-step.

Scan Big

Whenever you're scanning an image to be restored, you should always set the scanner to an output size larger than the size of the final image. There are several reasons for this. Mainly, it gives you more pixels to work with. Also, when you're finished retouching the image you can reduce it (called down-sampling) to the desired size. After showing you how bad an image can look after resizing, you may wonder why now I'm advocating down-sampling. In the previous examples, the size was increased (up-sampling). The process of down-sampling an image has a tendency to smooth an image.

The image we start with, shown on the right, was scanned and resized to 600 percent of the original size.

Even though the image was kept out of the light, over the past 30 years the color has faded. On top of that, color back then was not all that great. Even though there is no way to know precisely what the colors were in the original, we can use some of the tools in Paint Shop Pro to come up with a reasonable approximation.

Before starting a photo restoration it's important to understand that there is no fixed formula that works for all images. It is a matter of experimentation.

One Step Photo Fix

The One Step Photo Fix command in Paint Shop Pro is always a good starting point. It's a script that applies several common automatic corrections to your photo in one step. The result is shown next. If you're in a rush, you can stop here, but before we undo it (**Ctrl+Z**) and try something else, take a look at what didn't work with the One Step Photo Fix.

Two things draw my attention. The color saturation is low and the application of the contrast enhancement makes the pattern of the photo paper texture more apparent – not good.

Over the years I've developed an approach to restoring photos that may not be the best way to do it, but it works for me and maybe it will work for you.

The approach involves applying enhancements and corrections and using the Command History (**Ctrl+Shift+Z**) to jump back and forth between the original and the current enhancement. By jumping back and forth between the commands, you get a good feel for how different commands alter the image.

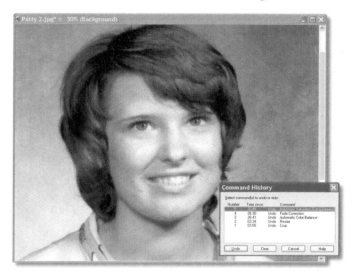

Command History offers the best way to do before and after comparisons during retouching.

The color balance of the original photo (right) is incorrect. As the reds in older color photos tend to shift towards pink, there's a color cast to deal with. In this case, the Automatic Color Balance (default setting with the Remove Color Cast checkbox selected) corrected the color enough so that the color of the background now looks like a common backdrop used by school photographers. Still, the photo appears faded and the application of the automatic contrast in the One Step Photo Fix didn't provide the right level of contrast.

In this case, the next thing I tried was Fade Correction. The default setting was too great so I tried several different settings until I had one that punched up the image without losing detail in the darker area of her hair (called the shadow region). After I applied the Fade Correction, I applied the automatic color saturation to increase the faded colors. The result is shown on the left.

Removing Defects

Once the color is corrected, the next step is to remove the defects in the image. That would be the blemishes on the photo that cleaning before the scan could not remove, the acne and the dark spot on her sweater.

The Clone brush can be used to remove all of the aforementioned defects. Your best approach may be to use non-aligned mode (selected in the Tool Options bar) and using a reduced opacity (roughly 70) apply the Clone brush in dabs. Because it's non-aligned, each time the clone tool is applied and released the source point for the cloning returns to the original source point. Another suggestion to use when applying the Clone brush is to use a source area that has colors or textures similar to the area you're trying to cover up (like acne). This way you'll avoid producing areas that stand out from the rest.

Removing Photo Paper Texture

Removing the texture pattern caused by the photo paper takes a little more time. Using the Smudge tool at a low Opacity setting, most of the photo paper texture can be removed, but it takes some time. It took me about 20 minutes to complete the overhaul of this photo.

With older photos containing lots of texture, you have the choice of removing all of it (which takes the longest amount of time) or you can use the Smudge brush to remove portions of it, which creates the appearance of the hand-retouched photos that were so popular in the late 50s and early 60s. Here's a close-up of the effect which, when displayed at 100 percent zoom, can look a little extreme. This is true of viewing all bitmap images.

The next step was to slightly darken the photo using the Gamma command and then selecting the Brush tool. Using the color white and a brush opacity of around 20, I whitened her teeth and the whites of her eyes. Usually the last effect applied is sharpening. When restoring older color photos like this, apply sharpening with caution, as it tends to enhance and bring out the very defects you were trying to hide.

Shown on the right is the final restored photo.

Scanning Printed Material

When scanning any printed material, make sure that you use the descreening feature of your scanner (if it's provided). Scanning images that have been printed can produce undesirable Moiré patterns that appear to be fuzzy checkerboards. If your scanner doesn't have a descreen

The best part about restoring those family heirlooms on a computer is that the photos won't ever fade again.

feature (not all do), use Paint Shop Pro's Moiré Pattern Removal command to remove the patterns. When it comes to scanning something from a magazine or a book, to get the best possible scan you need to remove the page from the periodical. If this cannot be done, then the next best approach is to lift the lid of your scanner or, if necessary, remove the lid (it lifts right off). Lay the book or magazine as flat as possible on the scanner and firmly (don't break the glass) hold it flat while the scanner scans. The edge of the material near the spine or stitching of the book or magazine will bend upward and may appear distorted in the scan. If it's necessary to remove the distortion, I recommend using the Mesh Warp tool in Paint Shop Pro.

Scanning 3D Objects

A scanner was designed to scan paper objects, but it can scan so much more.

For example, in the next photo, I scanned some counted cross-stitch work. The problem was that my co-worker Denise was still working on it. Since the piece wasn't stretched, it had creases on it and the lettering was a little distorted.

With Paint Shop Pro this wasn't a problem. While I could have used the Clone brush to remove the horizontal crease, here's a better way.

Use the Selection tool to make a narrow rectangular selection (with a small amount of feathering, say 3-4) roughly the height of the crease in the area of cloth directly above the crease. When the selection is finished, place the cursor inside the selection and while holding down the **Alt** key drag the copy of the feathered selection over the crease. The crease disappears.

To straighten out the slightly distorted letters, you can use either the Warp brush or Mesh Warp. While not perfect, here's the finished result. Ultimately the plan was to make a gift card out of the scanned image to accompany the handicraft project when it's given as a gift.

Much Larger Things to Scan

The cross-stitch piece was pretty thin. How about scanning something much larger? The next photo shows an antique Chinese teapot. To produce a record of the teapot for insurance purposes or to sell it on eBay, I could take photos of it, but getting that close with a digital camera involves a lot of set-up time and the flash may cause unwanted hot spots on the teapot.

Placing the teapot flat on the scanner glass with the lid open or off creates a dark image surrounding the teapot. While this scan could be used, the background is too dark making it difficult to create a selection around the edge since the dark background (caused by the lid being gone) and the dark metal look very much alike.

In the photo to the left below, I placed white tissue around the teapot. You could use any color but I chose the white as it diffused the bright scanner lamp. Now the detail around the edge of the teapot can be seen more readily.

This scan is good enough for insurance purposes, but if I wanted to display it on the Web, I need to replace the uneven white paper background with something else. Paint Shop Pro offers several different selection tools to isolate the teapot from the background. We explore this topic in great detail in the next section. Since the teapot had a very clearly defined edge, I choose to use the Freehand Selection tool set to Edge Seeker. After the teapot was selected, I copied it to the Windows clipboard and pasted it as a layer into a new image.

I used the Mirror command to flip it so it faced the other direction. The Flood Fill tool was used to fill the background with one of Paint Shop Pro's many gradient fills. The Text tool provided the vital information about the teapot. For the record: the information about the antique teapot is pure fiction. The teapot is a reproduction I picked up in San Francisco.

Tea pot, Chinese. Circa 2100 B.C.
Found in Zui Shan Prov 1993

Scanning, Copyrights and the Law

If you attend one of my scanning classes you'll hear a phrase I repeat often, "Just because you can scan something doesn't mean you are allowed to scan it." With the topic of copyrights making front-page news this year, I thought it important for you to be aware of what the law says about copying images. Here goes.

You cannot scan the beautiful photos that appear in most issues of *National Geographic* and sell them to others. I hope that's obvious. Now, let's consider a less obvious example. Let's say you hire a photographer to take photos of your children. Consider that you paid the photographer for his or her time, you paid for the materials used, and the subject matter is your children. Who holds the copyright to those photos? The photographer does. As such, it's illegal to scan the photos you bought from him and make copies. Along the same vein, if you're scanning images or objects for your scrapbook, it's also illegal to scan postcards, sheet music, commercially produced greetings cards, etc. — all of these are protected by copyright law.

Having said this, the enforceability of the copyright law in cases where you are scanning images for personal use falls outside the areas pursued by the respective authorities. For example, Hallmark will not be sending in US marshals with an arrest warrant if you scan in several of their new baby cards that were sent to you after your son was born.

Besides the issues of enforceability, copyright ownership becomes even more difficult when you cannot locate its owner. Case in point, I have a photo taken of my elementary school class in 1959 (yes, I'm that old). What are the chances of locating that photographer to obtain additional copies? About zero. Even if I found him, would he have the negatives from 30 years ago? Not likely. It used to be that all copyrights expired after 50 years and the subject of the copyright became public domain. In the USA, the expiration of the copyright has been pushed out under the Copyrights Term Extension Act (CTEA). Nothing copyrighted after 1922 has transferred into public domain. Why 1922? Because Mickey Mouse was born in 1923 in the movie "Steamboat Willie" and he was scheduled to become public domain in 2003.

My advice (but remember my entire legal education consists of watching episodes of "Perry Mason" and "Law & Order") is to be aware that almost everything you didn't create yourself is copyrighted. In almost all instances the scanning of these for your personal use — while technically illegal — can be considered OK. Just to cover myself legally, all of the text in this sidebar was printed with a special ink that will disappear an hour after you read it (I also watched "Mission Impossible").

Part 5

Making Your Photos Look Professional

It was a little over 103 years ago in February of 1900, that the Kodak Brownie camera appeared. For $1 the public had a camera that was so easy to use the ads said "the youngest children can take perfect pictures." The world has been taking photographs (both good and bad) ever since.

It's said there are two underlying reasons we take pictures: to forever capture a moment in time – birthday, wedding, graduation – and to prove we've been somewhere. There are many other reasons to take photos as well, but regardless of the motivation, we want the pictures we take to look good. If you doubt that, I challenge you to stand at a counter in a photo processing business. Watch a person's expression when his or her photos come out of the envelope looking good - or particularly bad.

With the Kodak Brownie and the millions of film cameras that have come and gone since, there's nothing that can be done after the shutter is pressed. All you can do is hope for the best and wait to see the results. With digital cameras, Paint Shop Pro, and Paint Shop Photo Album, each time you press the shutter, the creative process isn't finished, it's only beginning.

In this, the largest part of the book, you're going to discover how to make your photos look great and have a lot of fun in the process.

Photo Makeovers

This topic is about improving photos after they've been taken. We are going to look at several different ways to improve the overall appearance of the photo.

The first one we'll look at is a Christmas photo called "Sisters."

This family photo has an incorrect color cast that detracts from the photo.

What's wrong with the photo? It has a slight greenish color cast, which is usually caused by fluorescent lighting.

Accurate vs. Desired Color

When it comes to color everyone has a strong opinion about how to approach correction. One school of thought strongly believes the colors in the photo should accurately reflect the colors of the original subject. On the other side of the philosophical fence is the belief that the colors in a photo should look like we perceive them. By that I mean that oranges should be orange and lemons yellow.

Fix the Color First

The first step is to fix the color – always correct the color before doing anything else.

Use Paint Shop Pro's Automatic Color Balance (**Adjust > Color Balance > Automatic Color Balance**) first to see if it corrects it. In the dialog shown next, I have not selected the default setting but have instead used a saved setting that works with all the photos I took that morning.

To find the optimum setting I enabled the proof button and moved the slider to higher values until the green is gone but not so much that it develops a bluish color cast.

Automatic Color Balance in many cases can quickly remove the color casts caused by poor lighting.

To remove a specific color cast, I recommend using the Color Balance adjustment. Some users think this process is complicated. Let's look at it and I think you'll find it's not complicated at all.

If the Automatic Color Balance doesn't do the job for you, the Manual Color Balance provides the greater and more precise control.

Understanding the Color Balance Dialog

Looking at the Color Balance dialog, it's divided into the three color channels that make up an image: Red, Green, and Blue (RGB) whose names appear on the right side. The colors on the left side of the box are the complements of RGB — Cyan, Magenta, and Yellow (CMY). To remove a color cast, you must increase the amount of the color that is the opposite of what you want to remove.

In this example we need to reduce the green in the image. Looking at the middle slider, you'll see that we reduced the green by moving the slider to the left, increasing its complementary (opposite) color magenta.

In the photo above, you can see at the bottom of the dialog that the green correction was made only to the midtones (pixels whose brightness is neither dark – shadows – or bright – highlights). To complete the job both the Highlights and the Shadows must be corrected by selecting their button at the bottom of the dialog. While watching the photo, move the slider until your reference color looks correct. But what color should you use as a reference?

Finding a Reference Color

Here's the most important part about making initial color adjustments — don't use skin color to correct the color in an image. Flesh tones are complicated colors and you'll waste a lot of time moving the sliders back and forth getting them right. Instead look for something in the photo that should be white or near white, and adjust Color Balance to make the white part appear white. Once that's done, the flesh tones will usually fall in place.

Paint Shop Pro's Black and White Points command is also an excellent way to adjust color by indicating the highlights, midtones, and shadows on a photo.

In the photo shown below, I've identified areas of the photo that should and those that should not be used as references for making color corrections.

Finishing Up

Once the overall color is corrected so it looks right, the last step is to add a little punch to the photo. Traditionally, you could add a little contrast, but Paint Shop Pro has a neat little command called Clarify and it's like contrast on steroids. After applying Clarify to any image, you should consider applying the Automatic Saturation feature to punch up the color a little. With most photos, the last step is to apply some sharpening (Unsharp Masking or USM) to add a little extra sizzle. Photos of men and women over 30 are usually the exception to this rule since sharpening will enhance or otherwise bring out any wrinkles (not that any of these girls fall into that category). Here's the finished photo.

The photo looks better when the colors are corrected.

Paint Shop Pro also provides a large collection of interesting frames (**Image > Picture Frame**) you can use with your photos. Since the subject matter is pretty much centered in the photo, an oval frame like the one shown next, does a good job of directing the viewer to the subject. By changing the options on the Oval frame, it is possible to end up with a larger area at the bottom of the frame, which makes a good area to place descriptive text.

Christmas Day 2001 - Fremont, Nebraska

Tip:

When you are in the Picture Frame dialog you have several choices. An important one is whether or not the frame is inside or outside of the image. Since the Inside option covers the photo, look at both in the preview to decide which is best.

Accurate color is important if you're printing the logo for Nike® or IBM®. The colors in their respective logos are controlled with an exacting degree. Photojournalists also want the colors in their work to represent the captured event with as much precision as possible.

When it comes to the color photos we use every day, it's more important to make the colors of the subject look the way you want them to look. For example, if your close friend has a ghastly white pallor to her skin the day after the big promotion party, use the tools in Paint Shop Pro to make her skin appear less like a cadaver. Bottom line, make the colors in your photos look like you want them to look.

Paint Shop Pro 8's Black and White Points Filter

(The following suggestions about the Black and White Points filter are brought to you by Jasc Software)

The Black and White Points filter is an effective way to correct the color of an image or to match one image to another in a panorama. Though the filter offers a lot of flexibility, the simplest method of correction is pretty straightforward. Here is a photo we'll correct using the Black and White Points filter.

Accessing the Filter Dialog

To open the Black and White Points dialog, choose **Adjust > Color Balance > Black and White Points**. The dialog looks like this example on the right.

About the Filter

The basic idea of the filter is that you click a pixel in the left preview with an eyedropper to sample its color, and then set a new color for that pixel. The color you clicked is shown above the eyedropper as the Original color. The color below the eyedropper is the color that will replace the original color, or the Desired color. You can set this target color to anything you want by clicking the swatch and opening the Color Picker.

You can use one, two, or three eyedroppers to set the colors in dark, medium, and light regions of your photo. The colors you choose with the eyedropper are converted to the target colors you specified in the Desired color swatch. The other colors in the photo are also adjusted to match those choices. Click the eyedropper button under a color (Black, Grey, or White) to select it. You can cancel the effect of any eyedropper by right-clicking the button.

Using the Filter

The easiest way to use the filter is to click the Reset to default button in the upper right corner of the Black and White Points dialog. Then mark both the Preserve Luminance and Balance to Grey boxes at the bottom. Preserve Luminance means you only want to adjust the color of the image, without changing its brightness or contrast. This is the recommended setting when you are using the filter to correct color. Balance to Grey means you are going to set neutral colors (blacks, greys, or whites) to be truly neutral. Most images contain something that should be neutral and your eye is sensitive to tinges in such colors so you can easily make accurate adjustments.

If your photo has a color cast only in dark regions, start with the black eyedropper and click a dark area of the image such as a deep shadow. Do not click pure black, since you won't get an accurate correction. If your image has a color cast only in light regions, start with the white eyedropper and click a very light, nearly white area of the image such as a shirt or a window frame. For best results, avoid clicking on pure white highlights or flash reflections. For an overall color cast, use both of these eyedroppers in either order. If your photo looks good at this point, then you've done all that is necessary. If the colors don't look quite right, try clicking a different very dark or very light spot. Usually, no more than one or two tries are needed to find a good location.

After correcting the shadows and highlights for a color cast, look at the midtones for any residual cast. A good midtone region to look for is one with a neutral color that is lit indirectly. This might be a fold in a shirt, a button, a rock in a landscape, some concrete, and so on. Use the grey eyedropper to click this color and remove any residual color cast. This is normally all that is required to achieve a color correction.

Tip

The eyedropper can sample from one to 25 pixels depending on the current Sample Size setting in the Eyedropper tool. Setting a larger sample size is useful when you have a noisy image.

In the event your photo does not contain neutral colors of the brightness level you need, then uncheck Balance to Grey. Use the eyedroppers to click those dark, medium, or light colors about whose proper appearance you are certain. For example, you could click a T-shirt with a distinctive color, or a Christmas tree ornament whose color is familiar, or a sign of a known color, and so on. Hold the cursor over the sample swatch and check the color values in the tooltip that appears. Now click the target swatch and, initially, set the same color for the target. Finally, adjust the Hue of the target color away from its initial value until the image color looks correct. Complete the adjustment by tweaking the Saturation up or down if needed.

Tip

To display colors in tool tips as HSL rather than RGB, choose File > Preferences > General Program Preferences and on the Palettes tab select Display colors in HSL format

Other Ways to Use the Black and White Points Filter

Here are some other things to do with the Black and White Points filter.

- You can match one image of a panorama to another by setting a sample point in the first image and then sampling the target color from the same location in the adjacent image of the panorama. By keeping the Preserve Luminance and Balance to Grey checkboxes marked and using all three eyedroppers you can simultaneously match color and contrast between the two images.

- Do you have a photo that is beyond repair? Then try something wild. Unmark both checkboxes, use the black and white droppers to choose some colors, and then set some exotic target colors. Something uninteresting can turn into a colorful and exciting image.

- By clicking with the black dropper in light areas and with the white dropper in dark areas you can even make variations on negative images.

Color Correcting Old Digital Photos

My first digital camera had a 1-megapixel sensor and was one of the top cameras back in 1996. The top photo on the right was taken inside an office and it looks pretty bad.

When I used the Automatic Color Balance on this one, it had little effect. So, using the Color Balance command, I was able to quickly achieve the results shown in the bottom photo.

A real time saver for performing color balance corrections is to save your color balance settings by clicking the diskette icon in the upper part of the dialog and give each setting a descriptive name.

I've created about six office interior settings (with very original names, like Office Interior 1, Office Interior 2…) and many others for different conditions like early morning. I have almost a dozen for overcast days. When I opened the old digital photo, it only took a moment to go through the presets I had previously saved to pick the one that worked the best.

This photo was taken under fluorescent lights with a very early one megapixel digital camera.

Correcting the color is the critical first step.

Dealing with Noise in Digital Photos

Noise in a digital photo appears like fine grit. Photos taken under low-light conditions and photos made with early digital cameras produce a significant amount of noise. You can apply a light blur to the entire image and the noise will disappear (but the image will appear to be slightly out of focus). You also could manually go through the photo and apply the Soften brush to the noisy areas. This would work, but it's very time consuming.

Fortunately, Jasc put a clever command in Paint Shop Pro, Edge Preserving Smooth. It's a noise-reducing filter that, when used on photos of people, works so well at removing noise and wrinkles. It should be called a Botox® filter.

Cropping improves the photo even more.

Not all noise is bad. The presence of noise in a photo can give that part of the image an edge. In the office photo, the noise is most apparent in the faces of the ladies. To get rid of this, I quickly made a freehand selection around their faces and the one hand on the shoulder. This will limit the action of the filter to the faces and leave the noise content in the rest of the image untouched. After the filter is applied, the noise is significantly reduced.

At this point, the color looks better and the noise is reduced, but the background is distracting. We'll change that a little later.

Beware of the Flash

I wanted to stick in this photo tip so you'll have another option to consider next time you're shooting under low light conditions. The first photo was taken of the family Christmas tree using a flash.

The second photo was taken about a minute later. No tripod was used. I just moved back a few feet and rested the camera on the table and got this available light shot. Taking available light (no flash) shots of stationary images can produce pleasing photos.

Drawing Viewer Attention

There are several easy ways to change a photo to draw viewer attention to the subject. A unique method involves making everything in the photo black and white while keeping the subject in color. In the following photo of Bob the barber (age 84) the mirror reflections in the background are a little distracting.

We can make the background black and white and keep Bob in color — now Bob stands out from the background.

The best part about this technique is that it's so easy to do. Using a different type of photo, here's how it is done:

1 Open a color photo like the one shown.

2 From the Layers menu add a Hue/Saturation/Lightness Adjustment Layer

3 On the dialog change the Saturation to -100 and click OK. The entire image appears to be grayscale but it's just an effect created by the adjustment layer.

4 Select a brush tool and everywhere on the image that you paint with black makes the layer (and its effect) transparent. If you accidentally remove the wrong part of the layer it's not a problem. Just paint the area with the opposite color (using the right mouse button) and it will become opaque again. In the screen capture, you can see the Layers palette showing the darkened area of the layer mask.

To ensure the color doesn't bleed outside the lines of the color object, you should either use a small brush with a hard edge or do what I did in this image and make a selection around the subject.

> **Tip:**
>
> If you make a selection to use with this technique, don't forget to select the background. Make the selection, then select the Adjustment layer again. If you don't you'll be wondering why some of the selection tools don't seem to work right.

Here is the finished image.

The unique beauty of the flower's color is brought into sharp relief by using an adjustment layer to remove the color from the rest of the photo.

Using Depth of Field to Make Subject Stand Out

When you focus your camera on a subject, there's a specific distance in front and behind the subject that is in focus, while the rest of the photo is out of focus. This distance is called depth of field and when the background is out of focus, it draws the viewer's attention to the subject in the foreground.

The image below is a great shot of the kids, but the parking lot background is a little distracting.

You can make the background less distracting by using the Freehand selection tool, and making a feathered selection that surrounds the background. Then apply the Gaussian blur filter at a setting that slightly blurs the background. You don't want to make the blur settings too high or the blurring will occur around the edge of the selections and the subjects will have a halo around them.

Blurring the background slightly is easy and emphasizes the children in the foreground.

Replacing Backgrounds

In addition to blurring the background to make it appear out of focus, you can replace the background. It's simple to do and only takes a few moments.

1 Using the office photo we fixed earlier, it is a simple matter to use the Freehand selection tool (use Smart Edge type of selection) to select just the two women using a slight feather setting (1 or 2) to give them a soft edge.

2 Copy them to the clipboard (**Ctrl+C**) and then paste them as a layer (**Ctrl+L**) on another photo. Before I pasted the new layer, I slightly blurred the Background image with the Gaussian Blur so it wouldn't be a distraction.

3 I used the Mirror command to flip them horizontally so they would fit in the new photo better and used the Move tool to position them as shown.

Of course, there are other good reasons to replace backgrounds, like when you want to just play around with a photo like the bottom photo on the left. At the end of the book you will find a lot more on the topic of what I call photo foolery.

Combining Two Photos

In Part 2 of this book, I discussed at length the difficulty of capturing images with bright highlights and dark shadows and gave you a few tips on how to overcome this hurdle. Here's a third option. It involves shooting the same scene twice with two different exposure settings and then combining the two photos to create one image that accurately reflects both the bright highlights and the dark shadows.

By measuring the darkest part of an image and shooting a photo followed by measuring the brighter part of the scene and using that setting to take a another photo of the same area, it's possible to create two images that can be combined using Paint Shop Pro.

Here's a real world example. There is a great little area near Austin, Texas, called Hamilton Pool. A long time ago it was a limestone cavern and half of the roof collapsed creating a cool and shady grotto. Photographically the problem is that the grotto is always in deep shade and the waterfalls and other parts of the pool are in bright sunlight.

Here is how this image was captured:

The camera was set to Spot meter mode, placed on a tripod, and pointed into the darkest area of the grotto to take the light measurement. By holding down the shutter half way, the camera held the meter setting.

Take the First Photo

While still keeping the shutter partially pressed the camera was pointed directly at the falls and the shutter pressed the rest of the way down. Because the camera used the settings for the darker part of the image the resulting photo has the grotto illuminated correctly, but the area of the falls is completely overexposed.

In preparation for this photo, the camera exposure was set to measure the darker area in the cave grotto even though the sky was grossly overexposed.

Take the Second Photo

Without moving the camera, I released the shutter button and then took a second photo. This time the metering system correctly read the light in the brighter part of the image. That part of the image is correctly illuminated but all of the details in the grotto are lost.

Setting the exposure for the bright sky gives a properly exposed sky, but the grotto is in deep shadows.

Combine the Two Photos

Using Paint Shop Pro, it's relatively simple to combine the two photos into a single image. Here's how it's done.

1 Open both images in Paint Shop Pro.

2 Make one photo (doesn't matter which one) the active image.

3 Copy the entire photo to the clipboard (**Ctrl+C**).

4 Close that image – don't save changes when asked.

5 With the second photo active, paste the first photo you copied to the clipboard as a layer (**Ctrl+L**) onto the second photo – at this point all you can see is the top layer.

The goal now is to remove the unwanted portion of the top layer so all that you can see is the best part of both photos. There are several ways to do this. Using the Eraser tool we could just erase the part of the top image we don't want. The limitation of that approach is that anything we erase is lost and cannot be recovered. So here's a better way. We'll create a Layer Mask and modify it to control what parts of the top layer are visible and invisible. The advantage is that any part of the top layer made transparent by using the layer mask can be made visible again.

6 From the menu choose **Layer > New Mask Layer** and **Show All**. At this point nothing seems to have happened.

7 Select the Brush tool and make sure the default colors (black foreground and white background) in the Materials palette are selected.

8 Change the Opacity to approximately 50 percent and begin painting the mask layer with black (left mouse button) in areas where you want to fix the exposure. Every place you apply black, the top layer will become slightly transparent. To restore part of the photo, paint that area of the mask with white (right mouse button).

By combining the two photos I've created an accurate photo of what Hamilton Pool looks like.

Combining the two previous photos in Paint Shop Pro produces a photo that would otherwise be impossible to capture.

Adding Blue Skies and Fluffy Clouds

You can go beyond what was really there the day the photo was taken. Using the same technique that was used to combine the two photos we can replace the overcast sky with a nice blue cloudy one like the one shown below.

The major difference you will encounter when putting dissimilar photos like a cloudy sky and a landscape together is accurately defining the uneven edge of the cliff and shrubbery. This isn't that difficult since the overcast sky is almost pure white. Here's how to do it.

1 After pasting a photo of the replacement sky as the top layer, create a Layer mask and this time use Hide All. This will make the new sky disappear.

2 In the Layers palette activate the layer containing the overcast sky and use the Magic Wand to select the area to be replaced. You'll discover that it is difficult to get a good selection with some trees and shrubs because the Magic Wand leaves an edge of the old background around interior edges. Since these are not critical for the final image, I recommend that you use **Selection > Edit Selection** and remove them by painting over them in this mode.

3 After the selection is complete, in the Layers palette return to the Layer Mask for the sky and paint the area within the mask. As you do, the sky will appear.

Adding a sky from another photo makes a good photo into an outstanding photo.

Improving Composition

On occasion you either don't have time to properly compose a shot or don't see the composition of the shot until it is displayed on the screen.

The Crop tool is the initial tool for improving composition. The procedure is simple, deceptively so.

1 Decide what's the subject or focus of the photo.

2 Crop the photo to emphasize the subject.

Back in the old days, cropping was done with an Xacto™ knife. Once you cut the print there was no undo button. With the Crop tool you can Undo, or make multiple copies cropping each one differently. The combinations are seemingly endless.

Let's look at some real world examples of cropping.

When taking this photo, I was after a photo of the couple kissing and didn't see the boy hiding his face until I opened the photo in Paint Shop Pro.

The parts of the photo to crop seem pretty obvious: the pastor and his shadow on the left, the exit sign isn't very exciting either. At the same time you're deciding what part of the photo to lop off, there's something else to consider. Will the finished photo be printed and framed? This is an important question since frames comes in common sizes like 4 x 6, 5 x 7, etc.

So, if we crop the image without giving any thought to the finished dimension, we could end up with a photo that's difficult for someone to frame.

Cropping to Fit Standard Sizes

Both Paint Shop Pro and Paint Shop Photo Album allow you to set the resulting size of the cropped image. Here is how to do it using Paint Shop Pro.

1 Select the Crop Tool (R) and in the Tool options toolbar mark the Specify Print Size box. But note that the Presets contain many standard print sizes you can use.

2 Open Presets and select one of the standard size presets.

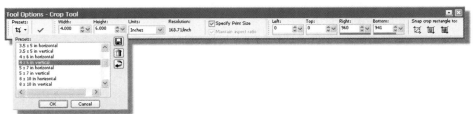

After you click the OK button a crop area rectangle appears on the photo. Don't pay any attention to the size. We'll change that in a moment. Position the crop area rectangle so it's roughly in the area you want to include in the final photo. Now grab any of the corners of the crop area and as you resize you'll notice the resolution in the Tool options toolbar continually change to ensure the final print is the size you selected. As long as the resolution stays in the range of 140 or greater your photos will print fine. If you like, you can enter the Width and Height settings directly into the Tool options toolbar rather than using the Preset.

Thinking Outside of the Box - Cropped Area

Let's look at an alternative to the traditional photo composition.

Tip

Beware of the desire to add just a little bit more. In this image the temptation would be to include the rest of her dress. If it has nothing to do with the subject matter – lose it.

Making Post Card Cut-Outs

One way to make the happy couple and family stand out from the background is to remove it all together. Here is how I did it in Paint Shop Pro:

1 Using the Rectangle selection tool I selected the part of the image that I wanted to use and then copied it to the clipboard (**Ctrl+C**).

2 Next I made a new image that was postcard size and pasted the clipboard contents as a Layer (**Ctrl+L**). Now that could work as it is, but let's see what else can be done.

3 My original idea was to have the bottom part of her dress draped outside the small photo inset. So, I used the Background Eraser tool (described later) and removed the background and the floor around her feet and dress. The result (shown below) was OK

but not what I had in mind. Also, there's part of the boys in the background that are cut off by the edge of the original photo.

4 I flipped the image using the Mirror command (**Ctrl+M**) so the flat edge of the kids would coincide with the left edge of the card. Then I used the Background Eraser to remove the remainder of the background. To make them stand out from the white background, I applied the Drop Shadow filter from the Effects menu at its default value. Now they appear a little like cutouts.

5 All that was left was to add the text.

Thanks for being part of our
25th Wedding Anniversary

Bryan and Debbie

Creating Action

Earlier in the book, I gave you some tips on capturing action with your digital camera. Now that you've captured the action, you can enter a new world of digital manipulation. This is an area that, up until now, has been limited to those producers of the fine art that serves as the covers of supermarket tabloids. Yes, with the right tools (Paint Shop Pro) and a little imagination, you too can create the extraordinary action photos that grace the covers of sports magazines and tabloids.

To demonstrate some of the things that are possible, meet my associate Paul. He's 12 years old and he's 100 percent boy..

Although this photo is full of action, it can be improved:

First: It was almost noon, the sun was bright and directly overhead. That's why there are dark shadows on his face and the back of him is a little washed out.

Second: The background is . . . well, ugly.

Third: Because the camera caught him mid-air both Paul and the skateboard look like they're floating.

Unleashing Your Imagination

The first job is to separate Paul from the background. I cover removing backgrounds quite extensively in the next section, so I won't cover it now. I used the precision Background Eraser in Paint Shop Pro to remove the background, leaving Paul floating around on a layer by himself. Next, I used the Canvas size command to make the background larger since we are going to make an action photo. I wanted him to have plenty of room.

By removing the background and enlarging the image using the Canvas command, we give Paul plenty of room to show his stuff.

Variation No. 1

The first variation involved using the Mirror command (**Ctrl-M**) to make Paul face the other direction. I replaced the background with one I downloaded from my favorite stock photo house (www.photospin.com). I put Paul immediately to the right of the white blur to give the appearance of motion. I wanted it to appear a little like the white area was pushing him out. It looks OK, but we can do a lot better.

Replacing the background with an artistic one like this gives the photo a professional quality.

Variation No. 2

The second variation involves duplicating the layer Paul is on, and creating two identical copies of Paul, one on top of the other. Next I applied the Smudge Brush to smear the pixels of the bottom layer. This way, the top layer remains unaffected, but the bottom layer is smeared creating the appearance of a blurred motion trail. Here's how it's done:

1 Duplicate the layer containing the action (Paul on the skateboard).

2 In the Layers palette, select the bottom layer.

3 Choose the Smudge Brush. You'll need to experiment with the settings to get the brush the correct size for your photo (bless the Undo command). This was a large image so I set the Size to 500 pixels (as large as it would go). The Opacity was set to 75 and the Step to 15. The setting that has the greatest effect on the illusion of the motion is the Step setting – so concentrate your efforts there.

4 For this effect, I clicked the Smudge Brush on his skateboard and then while holding down the Shift key, I clicked at a point in the middle of the left side of the image. By holding down the Shift key while clicking, Paint Shop Pro will paint a straight line from the initial starting point to the end point.

Now he looks like he was shot out of a gun. This is also a great technique to use on skiers who generally take great pride in their downhill speeds.

By smearing a copy of the Paul underneath the top layer, we can give the appearance of him rocketing off of the photo.

Variation No. 3

This variation is fun and easy to do. It mimics the effect of someone taking multiple exposures with a high-speed camera. Paul is still on a layer so we duplicate the layer three times leaving us with the original and three identical copies. I left him facing the original direction since, for this effect, I wanted him to end his skateboard run in the light end of the background. Placing each of the duplicates to the right of the original, I used the Levels setting in the Layers palette to make each duplicate progressively more transparent. Next, I used the Deform tool to rotate and deform the body in each of the copies so it appeared that they weren't copies but pictures taken at different times during the skateboard jump.

Multiple copies of the skater rotated to different angles and differing opacity levels produce the effect of a multi-exposure images that is very popular with sports photography.

Different Backgrounds

But you say, I don't have a subscription to a stock photo company and don't own any fancy backgrounds. No problem, make your own.

One way is to take background shots at similar sporting events. Just general crowd shots. To create an abstract background, you'll need to take a different approach. The following image was made in a café while waiting for a meal (always keep your camera handy). I snapped several photos of some bright interior lights near the ceiling (without flash) while moving the camera. .

This image would make an excellent abstract background. Since Paul was wearing a red shirt, I wanted to use a complementary color for the background. To get a complementary color (the opposite of red is cyan), use the Hue-Saturation-Lightness dialog. I turned the Texas Longhorn burnt orange into a blue. Next, I used the Mirror command (**Ctrl+M**) to flip the entire image horizontally before using the Twirl (**Effects > Distortion Effects > Twirl**) to create the background shown next.

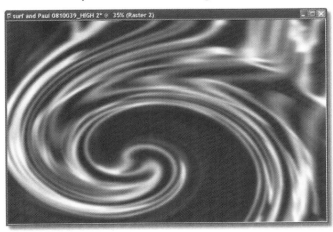

And here is a variation of the motion trail effect with the new background.

Creating your own background and swirling it also gives the effect of motion to the skater.

When creating the illusion of action, I want to encourage you to be imaginative - don't limit yourself. What would Paul look like on the cover of a magazine? It's an easy thing to scan in the cover of a sports magazine and reinvent the cover.

This doesn't prevent you from doing it for your personal pleasure. My favorite is to take covers of issues that have action photos and replace the professional stars with future sports legends. By the way, even though it's not an action shot, save your copy of *TIME* magazine's Person of the Year. It's always fun to put someone you know on the cover. Since I cannot show a doctored cover for copyright reasons, I thought I would make a magazine cover which, to be honest, was more fun than trying to match the look and feel of a real one.

Here is the original photo taken near his home.

Here is the cover.

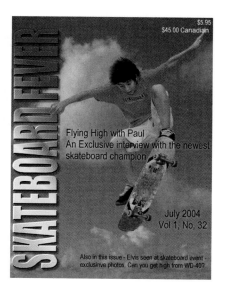

Finally, think outside the photo. You are not restricted to the sport the person is actually engaged in. For the last image I used the photo that I used for *Skateboard Fever* magazine.

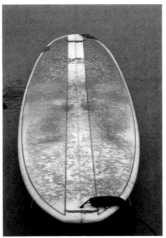

Having been raised in Southern California, I know that skateboarding evolved from surfing. So I found a photo I had taken of a surfboard lying on the beach and used the Deform tool, to change its perspective.

I also applied the Deform tool to Paul to create the right perspective. We live in Texas so the idea of surfing is rather remote (although I hear we get great surf on the Gulf of Mexico during a hurricane). The foam breaking under his surfboard was done by applying foam from another part of the wave photo with the Clone brush at about 70 percent Opacity so you can see through the foam and water a little.

These are just a few of the possibilities for action shots. As you can see the possibilities are almost limitless using Paint Shop Pro 8 and a little imagination.

Getting the Most out of the Precision Background Eraser

With the release of Paint Shop Pro 8 comes a powerful new tool, the precision Background Eraser. (Did the title give it away?) The *Paint Shop Pro 8 User Guide* describes the Background Eraser as a tool that can "...select a colored area of the image and replace it with transparency." This is an accurate description, but it only hints at what you can accomplish with the Background Eraser. So, let's start off with my personal, but unauthorized, description of what this tool does.

The name says it all. This tool erases the background of an image and does it extremely well. As you paint over an area, the Background Eraser reads the color information of the pixels underneath the eraser icon in the center of the cursor.

As you drag the brush across an image, any pixels inside the circle (which indicates the brush size) that are the same color or within a selected range (tolerance) of the pixels beneath the eraser icon are selectively made transparent. This is the continuous (default) operating mode. There are other modes that let you select one color and use it to replace all of the others. While this is nice, I rarely use these other modes. If you want to learn more about them, you can find more information in the *Paint Shop Pro 8 User Guide*.

After working with the Background Eraser, it has become my tool of choice for removing backgrounds. Since a picture is still worth a thousand words, even adjusted for inflation, let's look at some ways you can use this most marvelous tool.

Classic Background Removal

Meet three of my co-workers – Kathy, Janet, and Shannon (left to right). No, I don't work in a tropical food eatery; I took this picture during an office celebration of a project that had a tropical name. The background is cluttered and doesn't look very tropical. In a typical publishing situation, you have three choices: leave the cluttered background, select the background and blur it, or replace the background with another. I chose background removal and replacement because the edge formed by their long hair and tropical outfits makes a smooth continuous edge – mostly.

Here is how to remove the background:

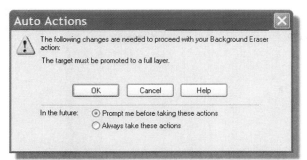

2 If your photo doesn't have layers, when you click the photo, a message box (shown here) appears asking your permission to make a layer. This Auto Action appears because pixels in a background cannot be transparent, so Paint Shop Pro needs to make your photo into a raster layer.

3 After you click **OK**, zoom in close on a part of the image you want to remove. I used the Background Eraser default settings with the exception of the brush's **Size** and **Hardness**. When working with hair, I recommend using a much softer brush (the default setting of 100 has all the softness of a bowling ball). Next, I changed the **Size** of the brush in the Tool Options palette so it was large enough that the center of the tool could be near the edge while the edge of the brush over-

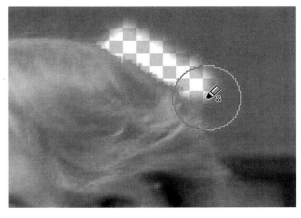

lapped the hair. I clicked at a point a short distance outside her hair and dragged the Background Eraser as shown. As the tool is dragged, the pixels of the background become transparent. Note that you must keep the center of the brush in the area you are using.

If the tip of the Background Eraser tool accidentally touches her hair, it is removed as well. If this happens don't use the **Undo** command like I did for so long. Jasc put a clever little feature into this tool just for such a situation. Simply right-click and paint back over the pixels and they will be restored. Because the Background Eraser is reading the pixels underneath the icon to ensure all the background pixels are erased, you may need to get the cursor close to the edge to read those colors.

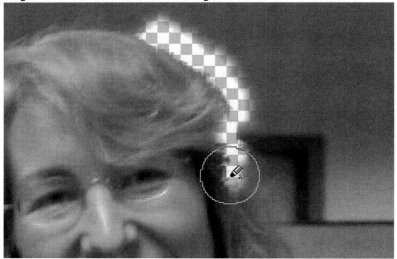

4   In this photo, I continued moving around the image – it only took about two minutes to create a transparent edge. After you have the edge defined, it's a simple matter to erase the remainder of the image using the standard **Eraser** tool. Actually, a faster way to do this is to make a rectangular selection over a part of the background you want to erase and use the **Delete** key to erase the contents of the selection. Repeat this action with various sized selections until only the subject remains.

5   Once all of the background is transparent, you have several options for placing it on a new background. You can copy the contents of the layer to the Windows Clipboard and **Paste As New Layer (Ctrl-L)** on a different photo. Or, open a new image and from the **Layers** palette of the original image drag the raster layer onto the new image.

Since all of the ladies in the photo appeared so tropical, I chose a tropical photo for the new background.

Another example of a background replacement that is a little more complex uses a photo I took of a butterfly. The poor little insect gets lost in the grass. So, I thought I would see how well the Background Eraser worked on a background like this and discovered that it worked surprisingly well. The only challenge I had was the butterfly's antenna. To get the antenna, I had to use a very small brush and zoom in really close.

This photograph of a butterfly is relatively uninteresting.

Without the Background Eraser it would be very difficult to eliminate the background and keep the tiny details like the antenna.

I thought the butterfly looked a little faded (it was photographed on a very bright day). Since one of the fun parts about having Paint Shop Pro is the ability to make images look better, I applied the One Step Photo Fix and it looked much better before pasting it on a different background.

I looked at several different backgrounds and didn't find anything that would make the poor butterfly stand out, so I took a photo of some flowers and in the Hue/Saturation/Lightness removed all of the color (**Saturation to -100**). Then I pasted the butterfly on as a new layer and added a slight drop shadow (**Effects > 3D Effects > Drop Shadow**).

To add even more interest, I used a Paint Shop Pro Picture Frame to add the final touch.

Removing Cast Shadows with the Background Eraser

Cast shadows are produced by your camera's flash and appears as those nasty dark shadows on the wall behind your subject. Here's a photo I took of Nick during the same festive tropical event. There are two challenges when removing the background from this photo. First, the cast shadow is close to the color of his hair. Second, he's wearing glasses, and we need to make the inside of his glasses transparent.

Cast shadows caused by using a flash are, in many cases, unavoidable.

When the foreground and the background are very similar in color (like the shadow and Nick's hair), you'll have greater success if you uncheck the Auto Tolerance feature in the Options palette and manually reduce the Tolerance setting to something between 8 and 10. Now, when the brush is applied to the shadow area, the Background Eraser doesn't erase his hair. But, it does leave some debris in the area that is supposed to be transparent. This is easily removed by holding down the spacebar (which turns the Background Eraser into the Eraser tool for as long as it's held down) and using the eraser to clean up any dirty area.

After finishing the area close to his hair, I used the Auto Tolerance setting for the rest of background removal, including the part of his glasses that should be transparent to the background. I found the best way to accomplish this was to click inside the area that needs to be transparent. The frames of the glasses and even the reflection on them will be preserved as you click around inside the frame. When I had finished with Nick, I also put him into a tropical setting. Notice that you can see through his glasses. I also used the Preset Shapes tool to give him something to say.

Removing Background from Inside the Foreground

The last background removing challenge we will look at has to do with background information that appears scattered throughout the subject.

Up until now, we have only used the Background Eraser to define a solid edge. Now, let's see how we can create transparency within the subject.

The photo I took of Morgan was against a boring brown brick wall, which can be seen through her hair. If we use the techniques used above, we would have a photo of Morgan with brown bricks in her hair. This is probably not the fashion statement she wants to make.

To remove the background from her hair, I changed the Background Eraser **Limits** setting to **Discontiguous**, changed the brush **Hardness** to 100 (bowling ball hard) and made the brush **Size** large enough so that the brush overlaps the holes in the hair. Now every time I clicked the background near her hair, all of the background in the hair is also made transparent.

After the background is removed from the hair, I changed the **Limits** back to **Contiguous** and finished making the background around her transparent. Just as with the other methods we've looked at, I finished removing the rest of the background and pasted her into another photo.

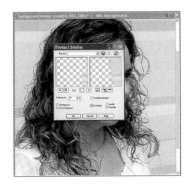

So, want to know the real secret to getting these great results with the Background Eraser? Practice. Pick out some of your favorite digital images and when you're not under a deadline to produce something, play with it. In a short period of time, you'll get the hang of using it – and you'll be glad you did.

In the previous sections, we learned some basic techniques on how to use the precision Background Eraser to replace backgrounds. If it were a perfect world, that would have been all you needed. But, in the real world, things rarely work the way they're supposed to and photos are never as perfect as they are in examples. So, I wanted to share some additional tips and techniques to improve the results you can get with the Background Eraser and some fun stuff you can do with it and your digital camera.

Cleaning Up Background Eraser Debris

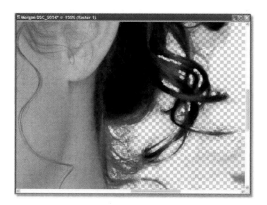

Earlier, we learned that when using the Background Eraser on parts of an image that are similar to the background color, it is often necessary to turn off the **Auto Tolerance** and use manual settings. The resulting transparent areas usually contain a lot of debris. You could zoom in and remove all of the debris using the regular Eraser tool. But, when there's a lot to remove, it becomes a daunting task. Here's a method that takes less time and cleans up most of the debris automatically.

Automatic Debris Removal

To clean up the debris, we'll be using Paint Shop Pro's **Remove Specks and Holes** feature. This little jewel is included to remove the tiny random pixels (specks) and small islands (holes) found in some automatic selections.

So, how does that help us? All we need to do is convert the dirty debris into specks and holes in a selection and Paint Shop Pro will do the rest. Here's how it's done:

1. Prepare the edges.

    I described this in the last section, but here's a recap. When the colors of the background and edge of the subject (in this case the hair) are similar:

    Turn off the **Auto Tolerance**

    Increase **Sharpness** to **100**

    Reduce the **Tolerance** (I recommend starting with **10**)

    Next, reduce the brush **Size** so the edge of the brush only slightly overlaps the edge you are trying to preserve.

    Now, Zoom in so you have plenty of area to work with and dab (don't click and drag) the brush so that the tip of the cursor is on the slightly transparent area you want to remove.

    Just concentrate on cleaning up the shady area. At such high zoom levels, you should notice right away if it is not going to look the way you desire.

2. Make a Mask Layer.

2 Make a Mask Layer.

With the image selected choose **Layers > New Mask Layer > From Image**. When the dialog opens, choose **Source Opacity.**

3 Choose **Make Selection from Mask** (**Ctrl+Shift+S**)

At this point, you should have the 'marching ants' selection marquee displayed. If not, press **Ctrl+Shift+M** to turn on the marquee display.

Since we're finished with the mask layer, delete it by selecting it in the Layer palette and clicking the **Delete Layer** icon. When asked if you want to merge the mask, click **No**.

4 Open the Remove Specks and Holes dialog (**Selections > Modify > Remove Specks and Holes**). Since the settings depend on the size of the original image, when the dialog opens, you'll need to experiment a little (This is why you shouldn't use the settings I use, I work on very large photos).

- To start, I'd recommend Remove Holes with a setting of 1000 pixels by 50. Increase the setting until the parts of the image you want to keep begin to disappear from the after preview window.

- When you think you have it set so it will remove most (never all) of the debris, click **OK**.

5 Invert the Selection (**Ctrl+Shift+I**) and press the Delete key.

Much of the debris will be gone at this point. Invert the selection again so the subject is selected.

6 Use Edit Selection (**Selections > Edit Selection**) to make any final edits.

Toggle Edit Selection off and copy (**Ctrl+C**) the contents of your selection to the clipboard.

7 Paste the clipboard contents into another photo as a layer (**Ctrl+L**) and you are done.

How Good is Good Enough?

As one who has made selections for several years, here are some points to consider when creating and editing selections. First of all, what colors are in the replacement background? If they are similar to the current background, then very little cleanup is required since the old background won't stand out from the new one.

Next, is the subject you're selecting the main focus of the final image or one of many (as in a group photo)? If the subject of your current photo is not the dominant subject in the replacement photo or will ultimately be made a lot smaller (to fit into an existing photo), only a little cleanup is required.

Lastly, is this a thing you are doing for fun or a work project? When it's just for grins and giggles no one will notice the debris around the edges. Clients, however, have very critical eyes.

If you'll be doing this kind of project often, I recommend you go through the procedure several times until you're comfortable with it. Then use the Script Recorder to record the procedure beginning with Step 2.

Remember that the actual settings used with the Remove Specks and Holes varies a lot depending on the size of the image. Save the script and run it whenever you need a cleanup.

Another Hairy Selection Method

There are times when I shoot a photo and know in advance that I'm going to want to replace the background so I have the subject stand in front of plain background that is different from the color of their hair and/or clothes.

Here's a photo I took against a white garage door. There are a few problems with my choice of a background. It's not a uniform color (different shades of white) and she's wearing white – what was I thinking?

Knowing you are going to replace the background in advance allows you to take photos in front of a relatively single color background.

While the Background Eraser tool could be used, let's look at another option involving several selection tools.

1 Make a Color Range selection using the Selection tool set to Rectangle.

- You can see I made a selection that included all shades of the background color (except for the dark seam near the top, which is too close to her hair color).

2 Now choose **Selections > Modify > Similar**.

- When the dialog opens, select a **Tolerance** value that selects most of the edges you want preserved.

- In the screen shot, notice that part of her blouse is selected as well as the background. Ignore these selections that are far from the edges since they are very easy to remove. Concentrate on getting most of the background without losing the detail of the hair.

- Make sure that **Discontiguous** is selected. I recommend selecting **Anti-alias** (Outside). Once you have the setting the way you want it, click **OK**.

3 After you have made your selection (you have selected the background), Invert the selection (**Ctrl+Shift+I**) so the subject is selected.

4 To remove the parts of her white blouse that matched the background, you can use Edit Selection.

- Since they are closely grouped, it's easier to choose the Selection tool and while holding down the Shift key (Add to mask) click and drag over the stray pixels you want to remove. Don't try and do it with a single action, make several small passes to remove them all.

5 Copy (**Ctrl+C**) the contents of your selection to the clipboard.

6 Paste the clipboard contents into another photo as a layer (**Ctrl+L**) and you're done.

Here are some examples of another selection I had made using different backgrounds.

Someone Turn on the Light

The last challenge I'll address is how to find a subject's edge when it's in the dark like in this photo of Debra. I used the internal flash instead of my external one.

This is a good photo, but the background is so dark that it would be hard to determine where her black dress ends and background begins.

So, how would you go about finding the edges of this one?

It is easier than you might imagine. Here's how it's done.

1 Choose **Layers > Adjustment Layer > Levels**.

  ■ When the Levels dialog appears, move the mid-tone marker (in the middle of the Input Levels) over to the left until the image lightens to where you can easily see the edges. You must have the Proof or Auto Proof button on to see the changes in the image.

Where did all of those people come from?

Funny thing about digital cameras, they do a pretty good job of capturing details in the shadows. All you have to do is pull it out, but that's another tutorial!

Using the Levels adjustment layer allows the photo to appear lightened without affecting the actual photo.

2 To select Debra, you can use your favorite selection tool.

  ■ If you're using an automatic selection tool like **Edge Seeker** or **Smart Edge**, make sure you select the layer she's on and not the adjustment layer. If you don't, these tools won't be able to automatically select the edge as you drag the **Freehand** tool around the subject.

3 With the subject selected, you can select the Adjustment layer in the Layer palette and delete it.

- Since Debra is wearing glasses, use Edit Selection to remove the clear area inside her glasses. On the part that is partially opaque, change the opacity of the Brush tool to around 50% so the area is only semi-transparent.

Using the Edit Selection feature allows you to fine tune the selection including the important part of making her glasses transparent.

4 Same drill as before, copy the content of the selection to the clipboard and paste as a new layer in another photo.

Here is an example of the finished work. The rules of photo composition suggest placing the subject so it occupies an edge third of the photo. And while rules are meant to be broken, in this case it is good advice.

Fun with Photos

We have covered a lot of topics in this part of the book, now it's time to let our hair down and have some fun. Here is a digital photo of Cooper, who is the first-born of a friend. I thought the photo would be a good candidate for general photo foolery.

Using the techniques discussed earlier, the background is removed.

Once you remove the background from the photo, you can do just about anything you want to.

Next, I found a beach photo and pasted it in as a new layer. In the Layers palette I dragged it to the bottom layer to make it the new background. Next, from my favorite stock photo house (www.photospin.com) I downloaded a bucket of ice.

The thought balloon is made using the Preset Shapes tool which is, in my humble opinion, the most under appreciated tool in Paint Shop Pro. This tool can be used to add all kinds of dialog to photos as shown next.

We could leave the Coop as it is, but the idea of him sitting on the beach with a bottle of bubbly seemed wrong. So, as a finishing touch I took a photo of a milk bottle and put it into the photo as a layer. Next, using the Deform tool I changed the size of the bottle (it was huge) and put it over the ice bucket before using the Eraser tool to remove part of the bottle to make it appear as if it was in the bucket.

Even More Photo Fun

Last week, I went to a garage sale and bought a few action figures. I placed them on the hood of my car and took some photos. This one's my favorite.

I removed the figure from the background using the Background Eraser and took a photograph of my son (age 27) and removed all but his face.

Copying and pasting the head as a layer, I used the Color Balance to match the colors.

So with all of the advertisements for the movie "The Hulk" in my mind, I opened the Hue Saturation and Lightness (Shift+H) dialog and. . .

Of course, any green comic book character needs a background and something to stick in his empty hand. I thought an industrial-sized bottle of perfume might be just the thing.

Unleashing the Power of Panoramas

I love making panoramas. It's difficult for me to write a brief tutorial on the subject since I'd like to take a week and produce a 200-page piece of work. Say the word "panorama," and most people think of broad sweeping landscapes captured using expensive specialty cameras. While it's true that a professional film camera designed to take panoramas costs between $3,000 and $5,000, you can take great panoramas with your digital camera. All you need is Paint Shop Photo Album and a few simple techniques.

To visually demonstrate the power of a panorama, this photo shows a beautiful cloud formation that signaled an approaching storm in central Texas.

As good as the previous photo appears, the panorama reveals the size of the coming storm.

Making a panorama is really quite simple using the Panorama feature of Paint Shop Photo Album. Here's how it is done:

1 Take a series of photos of the area you want included in the panorama, like the photos below. There are few rules about taking the photos that I cover in "Taking Perfect Panorama Pictures" later in this section of the book.

2 From the Album view, use Shift-click to select the photos to be made into a panorama and click the Panorama icon on the menu bar. The selected photos appear in a separate window. The order of the images (L to R or R to L) is usually not critical when there are only two or three photos in the panorama. If the photos are not in the sequence they are to appear in the panorama, click and drag the photos in the Panorama window so they are in the correct order.

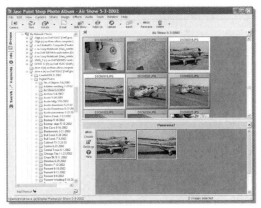

3 Click the Create button and the finished image will appear in a new window.

Photo Album automatically stitches the photos together and creates a selection for cropping the image. To complete the panorama, click the Crop button in the menu — the image is cropped and ready to save.

Look carefully at the number 5 on the plane. Sometimes two edges don't completely align. This effect of the semi-transparent duplicates is called ghosting. In most cases it can be corrected after the panorama is created by applying Paint Shop Pro's Clone tool.

Challenging Panoramas

Photos that are out of alignment or that have too large a change in perspective may not stitch properly. For example, when I attempted to create a panorama from the following four photos, it didn't work.

Here's the panorama created from the above images.

If you run into this problem, try removing one of the photos. In this case, the photo on the far left is the best choice because it's more out of line than the one on the right side. To remove the photo, right-click the image in the panorama window and select Remove.

In this case once the slightly out of line photo is removed, the panorama is created successfully.

For more information on the different settings for panorama, see the Paint Shop Photo Album User Guide.

This panorama was made from six photos taken in Athens, Greece, with a 2.1-megapixel camera.

I encourage you to give making panoramas a try. Panoramas are not limited to scenery. One of the original uses of panoramas was to capture group pictures which is great for family reunions.

Taking Perfect Panorama Pictures

Here are a few rules for taking pictures that are to be stitched together.

- Keep your camera level as you take the photos. The objective is to have all the photos align, as closely as possible, top-to-bottom.

- Try to overlap each successive image by about 50 percent. Increasing the amount of overlap beyond this will not improve the resulting panorama and can sometimes confuse the program.

- Expose photos uniformly. This is easiest to achieve if the light source (i.e.sun) is behind you. This doesn't mean it must be behind you, since many of the panoramas I shoot are of sunsets, which makes getting the sun behind you impossible.

- Find a point of reference. The Athens panorama above was made from six photos taken using a fence rail for support. Even though much is written about the need to use a tripod when shooting photos for a panorama, this example shows it's not necessary. Because Paint Shop Photo Album is good at aligning the photos, you can hold the camera in your hand. For handheld exposures, just pick a horizontal point of reference (like the horizon) and do everything you can to keep the camera level as you shoot. Another way to keep all of the photos level is to set the camera on something like a fence rail and rotate it.

Part 6

Sharing Your Work

"All who receive joy must share it; happiness was born a twin"
- *Lord Byron (1788 – 1824)*

Now that we have learned a lot about taking and improving photos, we come to the best part - sharing them with others. The options available today for sharing photos are amazing, if you stop to consider them. Assume that you just attended your daughter's graduation. Using your digital camera you take the obligatory photos of the new graduate in cap and gown with friends and family.

Armed with a memory card full of images you can do any of the following creative things to share the moment with others:

- Send photos attached to or embedded in e-mail.

- Upload the photos to an online photo service and have prints sent via mail.

- Create a slide show that can be played on a computer.

- Make a slide show on a CD that can be watched on TV with a DVD player.

- Post the photos on a photo-sharing site.

- Upload the best photo(s) to a service that puts the photo of the happy grad on calendars, greetings cards, note cards, and more.

- Publish your photos on a Web site (automatically).

At this point I thought it a good idea to show you how to do each one of these things.

E-mails and Pictures

Many users don't realize that there are different ways to send photos by e-mail. How you do it depends largely on who you send the photos to. Basically, there are three ways to send photos with e-mails.

- Attach the photo to an e-mail
- Embed the photo in an e-mail
- Use Paint Shop Pro or Paint Shop Photo Album to do it automatically for you.

Attaching a Photo

Depending on the software that you use to send and receive e-mail, attaching a photo is probably the simplest way to send a photo via e-mail. You compose the e-mail as usual and if you are using Outlook or Outlook Express select **Insert > File** and when the dialog opens select the file you want to send. The file will be attached to the e-mail as shown.

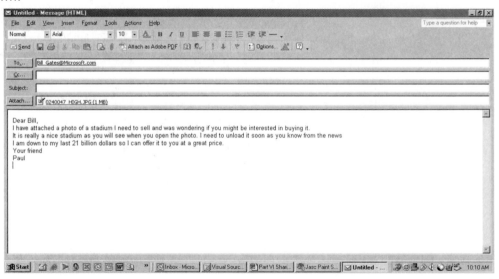

Depending on the software used to receive the e-mail (Outlook, AOL, or others) the attached file may be displayed at the bottom of the e-mail or appear as an attachment with the e-mail.

There are two things to consider when attaching a photo to an e-mail:

- Size of the image
- Modem connection speed of the person receiving the e-mail

Image Size, ISPs and Connection Speed

This is important since different e-mail services have built-in size limitations. At the time I'm writing this, Hotmail and AOL don't allow file attachments greater than 1 MB.

Whether imposed by your Internet Service Provider (ISP) or your recipient's ISP you need to be aware that attaching an image that is larger may result in the e-mail never arriving.

You should also be aware that sending someone a big file in an e-mail may be inconsiderate. Unless you know the person receiving the e-mail has a broadband connection (DSL or cable modem) sending a 3MB attachment to someone with a slow dial-up connection can take anywhere from 1 – 20 minutes. When your recipient checks his or her e-mail they'll have to wait until the entire image is downloaded as there isn't a way to tell the software to quit downloading a specific e-mail.

Other factors regarding image size also figure into how the photo will display on the recipient's screen. If your high-resolution 21-inch monitor is running at a resolution of 1280 x 1024 a photo that fits neatly on your screen will appear many times too large to someone running 800 x 600 on a 14-inch display.

What Size Should the Photo Be?

Whenever I send a photo in an e-mail, I always try to make sure it will fit the recipient's display so they don't have to scroll all around the display to see the image.

Here's a trick that I use when resizing images in Paint Shop Pro: with the image open in Paint Shop Pro, click the Fit to Screen button and the image will zoom to whatever value is required to fit the entire photo in the display area. In the photo on the right look at the percentage that appears next to the title. The image shown is displayed at 65 percent of its size. The size of the actual image remained unchanged, just the display size changed.

When I open the Resize command (**Shift+S**) there's a lot of information displayed in the dialog. The good news is we only need to look at a couple of values.

Original Dimensions – The dimensions and resolution of the image are displayed at the top of the dialog. Look only at the size expressed in pixels. Pay no attention to resolution or the size in inches (sounds like the famous line from the Wizard of OZ – "Pay no attention to the man behind the curtain."). At this point we're only interested in how the image will appear on someone else's display.

It's fair to say the lowest resolution monitor that you should encounter is 800 x 600 (SVGA). Most computers sold in the past four years run their displays at a setting of 1024 x 780 – or greater. Having said all that, I have friends that still use DOS on a computer with an amber screen monitor. You just need to decide where to draw the line.

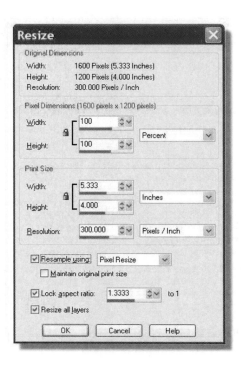

Pixel Dimensions – This is the section in the dialog that controls the percentage of change from the current 100 percent to the desired size. When the Lock aspect ratio box is checked – which it should be – you only need change one of the values and the other changes automatically.

When I change the Pixel Dimensions to match the percentage value that appeared on the image after I applied Fit to screen (65 percent); the pixel dimensions change to match the new size 1040 x 780 as shown. Even though the resulting resized photo would almost fit in a display running 1024 x 780 – there's a lot of other menus and things that are part of the normal Windows display that occupy part of the display area. So, while 65 percent would fit great on my display (I am running at 1280 x 1024) it would be too large for most displays. In this case, changing it to 50 percent makes the resulting file size 800 x 600 and for my purposes that's the right size. Admittedly, if I send it to someone running their display at 800 x 600 part of the image will be off the screen – but almost all of my e-mail recipients run at the higher resolution.

A common Resize misunderstanding to watch out for is "The Pixels Dimensions section is grayed out and I can't make any changes."

Check the box next to **Resample using** and it will no longer be grayed out.

Après Resizing

After resizing an image, you should always apply some degree of sharpening to compensate for the softness that resizing causes to an image. Don't go crazy and apply too much sharpening. For example, in Paint Shop Pro 8 the default setting for the Unsharp Mask (USM) command is set too high for smaller images that will be used on the Web. While I always recommend using USM, change the Radius setting to 1 and see if it looks OK. If there's still too much sharpening (usually indicated by the occurrence of tiny white specks in the image) reduce the Strength setting.

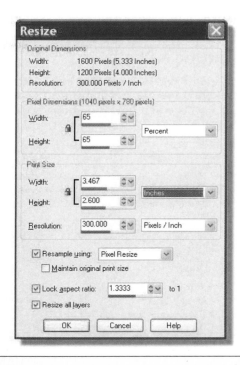

Note

The resize command remembers its last settings so the setting dimensions may not be 100 percent when the dialog opens.

Checking and Changing Your Display Settings

To check the display settings of your monitor, right-click anywhere on the Windows desktop and choose Properties from the bottom of the context menu. This will open the Display Properties. Click the Settings tab at the top and the current settings appear, as shown. From this tab you can change the Screen Resolution of your monitor. Down in the South we have an expression that goes, "You can't make a silk purse out of a sow's ear." In other words you can't set your monitor to a resolution it was never designed to handle – for several reasons. One, in some cases it could actually damage the monitor and another if you're using a

small display – like 14-inches – setting to a high resolution would make the displayed text all but unreadable.

Inserting a Photo

Many users are unaware that you can insert a photo directly into the body of an e-mail. The advantage of inserting (or embedding) the photo into the body is that you can control where and how the image appears in the email. Here's the same e-mail from Paul to Bill except it was sent using Outlook Express and the photo is inserted instead of attached.

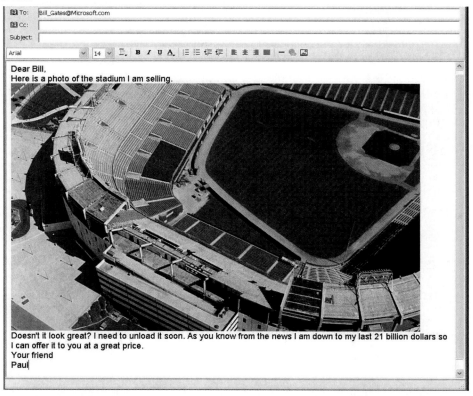

As cool as inserting photos in an e-mail appears, there are some limitations you should be aware of. First, if the recipient is running on a Mac platform, there's a chance they will not be able to see the photos – this is dependent upon the operating system (OS) that they're using. Second, if they're retrieving their e-mail using one of the many popular shareware programs (I find this is especially true among users of Linux) they too will be unable to see the photos embedded in the e-mail.

Two Methods for Sending Photos Automatically

Paint Shop Pro has a feature that will automatically open an e-mail with the selected photo attached. I covered this topic last for several reasons. First, it's a no-brainer. Choose **File > Send** and a Profile dialog will appear asking you for the name of your e-mail software – Outlook, AOL, etc. Click OK and the new e-mail appears with the photo attached. This leads to the second reason that I covered the topic of resizing images first. You see, Paint Shop Pro doesn't automatically resize the images. So you'll need to resize them yourself if they are too large.

Don't despair though, using Paint Shop Photo Album you can – as my granddad would say- "have your cake and eat it too." Here's how it's done.

1 Select the photo in the album that you want to send someone and click the E-mail button at the top of the screen.

2 The Profile dialog opens confirming which software to use to send the e-mail, and a new e-mail appears with the file attached – just like Paint Shop Pro except the photo has been optimized for e-mail.

You need to click the black triangle to the right of the E-mail button and make sure that it's set to Optimized images and not Original. The current setting is indicated by bold type as shown.

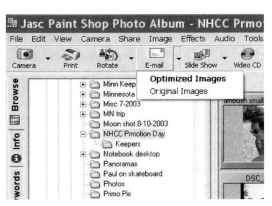

If not set to Optimized, the size of the photo remains unchanged.

Making a Slide Show

Rather than send individual photos to someone by e-mail, Photo Album makes it easy to create a slide show that plays on your computer. There really is nothing to it. Here's what you do:

1 Put all the images you want for the slide show in an album.

2 Drag them around inside the album until they're in the order you want. I recommend you play the slide show until it looks the way you want it. By the way, you can just select the images you want in the show from an existing album, (or by shift-clicking) without the need to save the entire album as a slide show.

3 Click the black triangle next to the Slide Show button and choose Save Slide Show. You'll be prompted for a location to put the slide show. Click OK and after a few moments you have a slide show.

Playing a Slide Show

After you have saved the slide show, here's how to play it.

1 Go to the location where you saved the slide show and you'll find a program called Player.

2 Double-click Player and it will prompt you for the name of the show that you want to play. Choose the slide show that you saved which will be a folder bearing the name of your slide show.

The key to a successful show is controlling the options on the show. You can set some of these options before you make the slide show by choosing Settings from the same list that appears to the right of the Slide Show button.

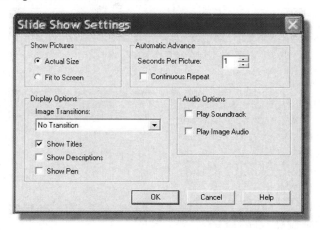

Here are some comments about the settings (most of these settings can be controlled using the Options feature in the Slide Show player).

Show Pictures – Fit to screen will enlarge smaller images to fill the screen. Larger images will always be shrunk to fit.

Display Options

- **Image Transition** - There are a lot of transitions that can be assigned to occur as the slides move from one to the next. There's one setting called Random that will randomly apply different transitions throughout the slide show. I caution you against using that one since some of the transitions require a lot of computer horse-power, and there's nothing that looks worse than watching any slide show program struggle in an attempt to get the complex transition accomplished. This is especially true if you are using Fit to Screen and allowing only one or two seconds per picture. Remember, your pictures are what the viewer wants to see, not the transitions. It would be pretty sad if when talking to a family member about how they liked the slide show they told you how much they liked the transitions.

- **Show Titles/Descriptions** – These options (if selected) show the description of the image and the title as shown below. The description and title are added to the image using the Info tab. If the Show Title option is selected and there isn't a title selected the program displays the file name. Regarding the descriptions, note that they appear in a small type. This may be an issue if you were planning on putting together a slide show and you expect people to be able to read the descriptions from a distance.

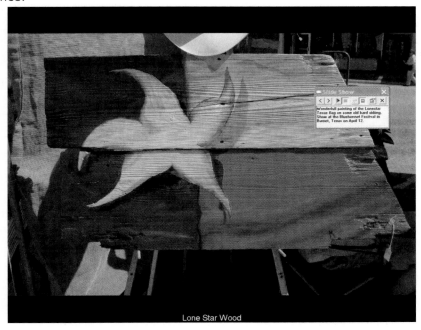

Lone Star Wood

Creating a Video CD

While you can put a slide show on a CD and play it on another computer, it is difficult to have the family all gather around the computer to watch – it's just not very Norman Rockwell. You can, however, save your slide show and more by creating a Video CD (VCD). This is a CD that can be played on most DVD players. I say most, because the early DVD players can't play anything but a DVD. Most of the DVD players sold over the past few years can play DVD, CDs, Video CDs, MP3 files, and more.

Creating a VCD requires that you have a CD (or a DVD) burner. The process of actually creating the VCD is quite simple and is amply described in the Photo Album User Guide. If you can't find your guide, when you start the process by pressing the Video CD button at the top of the Photo Album workspace, the screen shown next appears complete with a Getting Started Guide that takes you through the six-steps involved in making the VCD.

Another advantage of making a VCD is the ability to select one of many different backgrounds in the VCD menu. You can also create title pages.

Title Pages

One note about using the title page feature, which is one of the options in the Slide Show menu. Title pages are designed to provide titles and not lengthy descriptions. Each title page can contain three lines of text and since the font of the text is fixed when you get to the end of the text line, you will hear a beep indicating you should click into the second text entry line.

On top of that, you can add your favorite songs to use as background music as the slide show plays on the

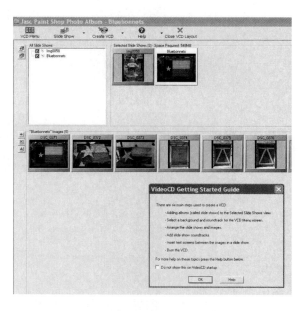

DVD player. Keep in mind that you're not just limited to music. One possibility for a family newsletter is to record different family members speaking and then save it as a sound file (MP3 or AVI) and attach that as the background music.

Publishing on the Web

With Paint Shop Photo Album, you'll discover that publishing on the Web is pretty simple. Here is what you need:

- A Host – This is usually your Internet Service Provider (ISP). Most offer a modest amount of disk space where you can post your Web pages. Most people have it available and don't even know it.

- Paint Shop Photo Album

Ah yes, I can hear you saying it's easy for you but how about me? Big surprise, when it comes to publishing on the Internet I am as dumb as a bag of hammers – really. Until last year I thought HTML was an acronym for some military weapon like Hyper-Light Missile Launcher or Heavy Tank Melting Laser. You can imagine my disappointment when I discovered that it stood for Hyper Text Markup Language. – go figure. For the record, HTML is the language used to make Web pages and it is a language you'll never have to learn since Photo Album does everything for you.

Make Your Own Web Page

Here's how to make your own Web page:

1 Put all the photos you want to publish on the Web in an album like the very short wedding album shown in the top right.

2 Open the Web Publisher (**Ctrl+Shift+W**) and a new window will replace the previous Album window. The selected photos will appear in the last used template. In this case I had selected the Wedding template as shown.

3 The last step is to click the Save button. From here you can either save the file to the hard drive or you can have Photo Album upload it to your Host. If you haven't uploaded anything before, you'll need to provide information to the program so it can upload the Web page. The next page (bottom right) shows the information that must be provided. You can get this information either from your ISP Web page or call one of their technical support people.

4 With all the technical information filled out, Photo Album can upload the completed Web page to your Host. When it's finished uploading the Web page, it will display the URL needed to open it from the Internet.

With this particular template, all the photos appear as thumbnails. Clicking a thumbnail changes the screen so a full photo appears, as shown below. Other templates operate in different fashions.

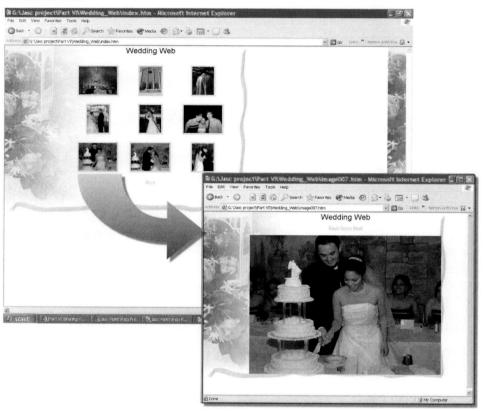

Conclusion

I hope this book has given you many ideas for your own photo projects. Now it's your turn to let your imagination soar. I sincerely hope that your journey is filled with photo opportunities to last a lifetime.